Business for the 21st Century

Business for the 21st Century

Towards Simplicity and Trust

François Dupuy
Partner, Mesa Research, California

Translated by Rupert Swyer

First published 2011 by
PALGRAVE MACMILLAN

Palgrave Macmillan in the UK is an imprint of Macmillan Publishers Limited, registered in England, company number 785998, of Houndmills, Basingstoke, Hampshire RG21 6XS.

Palgrave Macmillan in the US is a division of St Martin's Press LLC, 175 Fifth Avenue, New York, NY 10010.

Palgrave Macmillan is the global academic imprint of the above companies and has companies and representatives throughout the world.

Palgrave® and Macmillan® are registered trademarks in the United States, the United Kingdom, Europe and other countries.

ISBN 978–0–230–29263–5   hardback

This book is printed on paper suitable for recycling and made from fully managed and sustained forest sources. Logging, pulping and manufacturing processes are expected to conform to the environmental regulations of the country of origin.

A catalogue record for this book is available from the British Library.

A catalog record for this book is available from the Library of Congress.

10   9   8   7   6   5   4   3   2   1
20   19   18   17   16   15   14   13   12   11

Printed and bound in the United States of America

Thank you Dominique and Camille.
Sociology owes you a debt of gratitude

Contents

Introduction

Why write about the everyday life of companies and *in* the workplace at the beginning of the twenty-first century? Because I believe it is urgent to do so, given the gulf that has opened up between what is said by and about organizations and things as they really are.

Speaking the language of ideology

On the one hand, there is the language businesses use, especially when talking to their employees: their language quickly lapses into abstraction and coded allusions. In a word, it is ideologically tainted. It comes as a great surprise to the outside observer to note the complicated relationship (to say the least) that these organizations have with reality. Complex reality strikes fear into organizations, because it is not what they would like it to be. So organizations 'filter' their apprehension of it through stock phrases, weasel words, code words and a body of terms and notions, some of them very vague, which the system's actors ritually bow down to; the less they relate to reality, the more unquestioningly they swallow them.

Organizations speak of 'values', for instance, regardless of whether they truly reflect actual, recurring behaviour or whether their management systems (those famous 'HR policies') actually foster those values. They issue charters spelling out 'management principles', an idealized vision – or mere 'marketing' for external consumption – that bears little relationship to the everyday work of the people concerned. In other words, the actual constraints on collective action, and its essentially systemic nature, are denied in favour of soothing declarations or,

1

worse, notions that hold individual behaviour responsible for things that are in fact simply due to a lack of understanding of how human groups really function.

Obviously, this can work only up to a point! This suggests to me that some of modern management's buzzwords are destined to vanish as quickly as they arrived, with no mourners. Take the terms 'leader' and 'leadership', for example: I wouldn't stake much on their future. Yet today's managers bring them up at the drop of a hat. There's barely an executive training programme worth its salt that doesn't tout 'leadership for (this or that)'. This is a goldmine for consultants, coaches and specialists of every type. Yet, on closer inspection, the more people focus on the 'leader', the weaker their grasp of the complexity of collective action is. However, it is precisely the responsibility of the leader to understand and master the activity of the group. Unable to cope, leaders prefer to train their subordinates in leadership, hoping their individual qualities will compensate for the lack of any reasoning built on the way in which human organizations actually work.

What better illustration of this than the widespread fiasco of project management in the car industry and the subcontractors of that industry especially? Functioning in 'project mode' (a good example of management-speak) means deciding that, to construct a project or 'solution', one needs to bring together a cross-functional collection of actors hitherto content to work in their 'silos' or *'métiers'* (i.e., their trades, specialities or crafts). In a word, one 'de-layers' some of these and gets them to work horizontally, under the management (leadership) of a 'project manager'. The rest depends on the latter's managerial capacity to execute the project successfully.

Forgive me if this sounds brutal, but this betrays an intellectual laziness that pervades the life of modern business, no doubt a *quid pro quo* for the growing harshness of life in the workplace. The hope is that the personal qualities of the man or woman in charge of this peculiar way of working will suffice to make the operation a success. This is not the case, of course, and the most tangible outcome is to make it ever harder to find volunteers for this function of 'project manager'. Needless to say, this is not just a vague question of 'leadership', nor it is a 'technical' matter (as in project management techniques). What is at issue is the nature of the real power available to the project manager for dealing with the 'business lines'.

Here we leave behind the rhetoric of management to broach the basic *knowledge* that underpins the workings of the organization. To sum up: if this project manager has no meaningful 'control' over the actors assigned to him, he is powerless; he will get nothing out of them except by negotiating tenaciously and 'politically' for a sliver of their goodwill. From a managerial standpoint, he will not be a good leader. If, on the contrary, the career prospects or the variable pay of those assigned to the project depend on the person running the project, then he may have some prospect of success. This is not about individual leadership: it is a question of the organizational resources made available to the actors involved. In a word, it is about power relationships.

As the world of the enterprise grows ever more ruthless – something to which we can all attest and whose causes I shall be spelling out in this book – this 'intellectual deviation', which also produces feelings of guilt in those affected and renders those practising it unaccountable, will be less and less tolerated. I am willing to bet that one effect of the crisis the world has been going through for over 30 years now will be to 'twist companies' arms' and force them into using a little more realism in the way they do things and in the vocabulary they use to explain them. As we shall see in the final section of this book, some are already going down this path, which is the path of wisdom.

A theoretical and abstract language

Meanwhile, the way outside observers talk about the workplace is scarcely more encouraging. They have little understanding of life in the workplace because most of the time their knowledge is *spontaneous and/or ordinary*,[1] for want of an appropriate analytical framework. Business school professors in particular have largely contributed to the emergence of an abstract management language, though this is scarcely surprising since it is the same institutions – and to some extent the major English-speaking consulting firms – that rationalize *ex post* the simplistic practices we can observe in business. The ossification of the social sciences over the past 40 years or so in the United States, which was the birthplace of the 'management sciences' (we can hardly call them 'disciplines'!), has had a hand in this. Having become quantitative at best, and normative and prescriptive at worst, they too have lost their grip on reality, presenting statistics only very remotely related to what actors themselves actually experience, explaining to them what ought to be for want of understanding what is.

Sociologists must pluck up the courage to say that economists – especially those interested in work – have largely helped steer the literature on the workplace back in the direction of real life.[2] The most convincing work has been on the themes of work and what are known as 'psycho-social risks',[3] including those works by a handful of sociologists who have long been working in isolation. Indeed, this provides an opportunity to highlight, perhaps a little naïvely, how long businesses and government have taken to respond to the repeated warning signals sent out by specialists. Deteriorating working conditions, sometimes with dramatic consequences, are a striking example of this. There may be something of a vicious circle here, and admittedly the literature on the workplace scarcely makes for thrilling reading. Thus, its findings go unheeded ('it reminds me too much of the office'). Serious, well-argued warnings are lost in a welter of books put out by specialized publishers riding the wave of fashion.

Companies no longer have any idea what they are doing

However, and this is another warning I want to sound throughout this book in the faintly optimistic hope of being heard: companies have lost, or are in the process of losing, control over themselves. In the most direct meaning of the verb 'to know', they no long know what they are doing. That would not be particularly serious if it did not have direct consequences on their performance and, ultimately, on society. We will see that this loss of control is the result of a two-fold process that public and private organizations alike have failed to master, doubtless for want of having understood it, and also because they have no notion of what is happening right now.

To sum up: the period known in France as the *'trente glorieuses'* (the 30-year period of rapid growth between the end of the Second World War and 1975) set the scene – for reasons I have discussed elsewhere[4] – for a large dose of 'managerial sloth'. Companies surrendered control over whole swathes of their business; this applied both to their own units as well as to control over their clients and over the real quantity of work done by their employees. There was a time when the abundance of resources, especially those levied on the Southern hemisphere,[5] allowed companies to absorb their spendthrift ways without undue difficulty and to buy peace in the workplace, a commodity much appreciated when the economy was growing. During that blessed period in folk memory, shareholders were in alliance with their employees at every level (executives, as well as blue- and white-collar workers) for as long as they could be 'bought', thanks to what economists call the 'mark-up', in other words making a profit from their consumers. Interestingly, this 'sloth' (or exploiting this opportunity) was at work in all sectors of the economy ... even among Bordeaux winegrowers![6] It is this same 'sloth' that enabled the emergence of what we have called 'pockets of under-working',[7] an ever-present reality, yet one that is consistently passed over in silence, so persistent is it in the life of our organizations.[8]

But as conditions grew tougher, i.e., in the wake of the first oil crisis in 1974, it grew harder to continue in this consensual, though in many ways prodigal, manner. The pendulum had to swing the other way and means had to be found to assert control over what everyone was doing. In management's delightful vocabulary, organizations had to be put 'under tension'. More seriously, 'integration' became a major management concern.

Throughout this book, I therefore also want to explain what the seemingly banal term 'integration' actually refers to and, above all, I want to take a closer look at the 'tools' used to bring everyone back in line and, as it were, signal the end of managerial 'playtime'. Letting work 'take its own course', whether by giving people their autonomy or through low productivity, is a *contextual* practice: it is dependent on the economic circumstances that make it possible, and there have been few of these in history. Indeed, this is why those that have benefited most from this '*laissez-faire*' approach – civil servants, for example, though not only them – fought to get this privilege enshrined in so-called 'statutes' as a way of 'decontextualizing' it.

The optimistic predictions of the historian Fernand Braudel notwithstanding, the future is unlikely to favour this easy-going attitude to the same extent. The road back is likely to be a long one – taking the amount of time needed to realize that the techniques employed are pretty ineffectual – and could become steeper still. This is scarcely surprising, given that, from Taylor to Orwell, the history of the company – and of the world in general – has been dominated by efforts to pin down people's behaviour, or to keep it under control as they say in the world of business.

In order to do this, and regardless of the term used, people resort to various forms of *coercion*, a word unfit for polite conversation. Coercion is the exponential production of procedures or 'processes', reporting systems and indicators (e.g., Key Performance Indicators – KPI) to give the most familiar examples. The trouble comes when the system takes the bit between its teeth, with each level of the firm adopting strategies aimed at accentuating this tendency in order to be part of what they see as their organization's 'dominant mode', whether present or future. As we shall see, though, the cure is worse than the disease, and thanks to – or above all because of – managers' herd instinct, companies are descending into a lose-lose situation with their employees of all grades. This is because unless these techniques are handled sensibly, they create anxiety, disarray and suffering among those 'subjected' to them.

Instead of 'motivating' employees and inducing them to 'commit' to their company, these techniques fuel withdrawal and rebellion, whether active or passive. The phenomenon has now been clearly identified and analysed.[9] The more the company tries to control employees and put them 'under pressure', the more employees – including those in executive grades – seek refuge in alternative activities such as family life to compensate for the harshness of the world of work.

Better still: so contradictory are the elements of this crazy welter of processes, reporting systems and indicators that they end up carving out new areas of freedom for these employees, leaving actors free to decide which to apply and which to ignore. In a way, as we shall see, companies that fail to curb this proliferation sometimes give the impression of falling into the worst excesses of government administrations down the ages in the belief that one can predict and control what the different actors do by issuing rules, here in the generic sense. In the case of the civil service, the idea is to treat all citizens equally (the bedrock of our democracies)[10] and, in business organizations, to exercise control over their own functioning. We know how that works in the civil service, which ought to serve as a warning in the market sector...

Therefore, the aim of this book is to draw companies' attention to the fact that most of them are on the wrong track and to how they can do things differently. To prove this, we need to take a 'trip' inside these companies not as a tourist, but as an observer able to rise above 'ordinary knowledge', whose limitations are now clear. This journey takes us through 20 or so 'cases', each a veritable expedition into the world of the company. These cases grow out of a series of expert appraisals I have conducted in organizations of all kinds over the past five years. Needless to say, these slices of daily life in organizations and individual cases are reported anonymously. The places and sometimes even the sectors of activity have been altered. There are two reasons for this: first, I have taken a kind of oath of professional secrecy vis-à-vis these companies, and indeed I have signed a 'confidentiality agreement' with some of them; second, I have guaranteed total anonymity to the 800 or so people interviewed (who I wish to thank warmly) in the course of these expert appraisals. To make the account of these expeditions livelier and more telling, I have included excerpts from these interviews. To be clear, these interview excerpts serve to *illustrate* my analysis. They are not the analysis itself. To ignore that would be to confuse facts with anecdotes – precisely what is wrong with 'ordinary knowledge'. Even where cases are cited to illustrate a precise point, they need to be taken as a whole, and it is the whole that illuminates the parts.

Added to this is the fact that the reality we are about to explore is diverse and varied. The world of work is not a world in black and white. It is often contradictory and is always full of contrasts. This is why, inside a single company, we can find some of those famous 'pockets of under-working' alongside areas of 'over-working', which sometimes proves to be a breeding ground for psycho-social disaster. Consequently, the life of these organizations does not lend itself to ideological interpretation, at least not through our prism, that of micro-sociology. On the contrary, ideology, and the ideology of management-speak in particular, conceals reality; to use a once popular expression, it stops us from 'listening'. In contrast, the prime aim of this book is to listen to organizations and to those who work in them. Thus, I intend to report everything I have seen, which is not to say I have seen everything, of course. I merely hope that the spectacles I have used, those of the sociology of organizations, will help me to avoid distorting the worlds I have observed, some of which are quite surprising. One final note: in practically all of the cases I have studied, companies have called me in only when something has 'gone wrong'. The days when sociologists were invited to come and conduct a survey 'just to see what's going on' are long gone. An immediate consequence of this is that these case studies are far more likely to reveal problems (which is what the client wants) than to paint a trouble-free picture of life in the workplace. That is how these things work. Nevertheless, in the final section of the book, I take a look at how organizations that have managed to 'do things differently' function, anticipating rather than being subjected to the changing world in which they operate. This means that the book will at least end on a 'positive' note, as they say in management-speak, no doubt to ward off the evil eye.

Part I
How Companies Lost their Grip (1): 'Managerial Sloth' and its Consequences

1
We Have Let Work 'Slip'

A word on this notion of 'managerial sloth', to begin with, since it may give the impression that yesterday's people were less courageous or less aware when it came to managing organizations than those of today. This is obviously not so. Quite simply, each generation of managers works in a very different set of economic circumstances from the previous one, and this largely explains the choices they make. To make a comparison: in the 1970s, there weren't feckless governments on the one hand and virtuous ones on the other hand – they all faced tough constraints and adapted their policies in consequence. Day-to-day judgements on those policies were either polemics or *ex post* analyses of their consequences.

Managerial practice obeys the same logic. When the context or circumstances allow, practice adapts and, depending on the nature of the firm (public or private), it will focus more, first, on seeking to reduce situations of conflict within the organization than on maximizing gains. This is understandable insofar as, in our countries, the former (reducing conflict situations) is regarded as the condition for the latter (maximizing gains). Peace on the labour front and 'avoiding making waves' are the twin wellsprings of economic development in times of growth.

This is why organizations concentrated on developing their *endogenous* character, sometimes to a very high degree, for as long as possible (until some time during the 1980s). What this means is that, consciously or unconsciously, the first priority in building the organization, i.e., in the way people were expected to work, was to focus on solving its own internal problems – technical or human – as opposed to its environment, particularly its clients or 'users'.

We instantly understand that government departments are 'inherently' endogenous, insofar as the rules and principles by which they operate, especially in managing their personnel, are designed to protect their members first and foremost, rather than to 'serve' their relevant environment. There is no point in citing here the abundant literature or the many examples illustrating the subject. One has merely to read the reports of the French State Audit Court (*Cour de Comptes*), the only institution few in France would question when it raises these issues, to grasp the scale of the problem. If that is not enough, take a look at the mechanisms for the allocation of human resources in the French Ministry of Education or the police. A prime minister once suggested adapting police working hours to those of delinquents. He understood how endogenous these organizations are.

Externalities

Intimately bound up with this first notion is a second one, that of 'externalities', which I have developed with my colleague Jean-Claude Thoenig.[1] It encapsulates the simple observation that the actors in an organization (or 'system') are more likely to resolve possible divergences of interests if they can 'externalize' (or push) the cost on to their environment, i.e., the client or user, once again. Actors in government departments, for example, politicians, senior civil servants, lower grade staff and the unions, have a better chance of reaching agreement on working conditions and procedures if they can externalize or transfer the costs of their arrangement to the wider community via taxation or their monopoly position. Conversely – and this brings us back to the notion of context – this agreement is at risk of collapsing should public funds dry up, when markets open up or, more recently, when the rating agencies start raising their eyebrows.

Let's take a closer look at how these two notions of endogeny and externalities work in practice.

In the first place, people are not required to do much real work, and so labour productivity is low. The title of a recent French bestseller, which caused something of a scandal – *Hello Laziness*[2] – is deceptive since, taken at face value, it ascribes the responsibility for unproductive work to the actors themselves, even suggesting that they are deliberately slacking. Actually, I would prefer a title like *Hello Laxity*, since this slackness stems much more from tacit agreement among the parties than from any negligence or ill will on the part of one of them. In a word, you get the work you deserve!

The mechanism has been, and still is in certain sectors, the same in both the public sector and the private sector. As long as the external constraint is weak, either because the firm enjoys a monopoly (is in a de facto cartel) or because its margins are comfortable enough to absorb the cost of slacking, improving or even controlling productivity will not be the organization's priority. It will gladly buy social peace if others are going to pick up the bill, both in terms of direct costs (through the price they pay) and indirectly (through the quality of the goods or services provided). This gave rise to situations the uninformed observer would think 'absurd' when stated baldly. But they were everyday 'normality' for those involved. In the wake of the heatwave in France in 2003, the government ordered employees to work one unpaid day to pay for the cost of additional health cover for the elderly. In practice, bemused peak-time television viewers were treated to the spectacle of the head of a large firm explaining that, for his employees, the extra day would take the form of a few extra seconds per day! The corporate boss wasn't taking much of a risk, since no one has conducted a global study of the phenomenon of under-working. Only a handful of companies, obviously as a result of the pressure of necessity, have set about assessing the scale of this phenomenon, but they are careful to keep their findings close to their chests, for fear of setting the cat amongst the pigeons.

To be viable and, in truth, to avoid giving the impression that things really have spiralled out of control, this type of situation demands an 'adjustment variable'. In both the public and the market sectors, this is supplied by an army of temporary and short-contract workers of all kinds. The precariousness of their situation too is a kind of externality. What allows those with 'tenure' to pile up benefits of all kinds, both official and implicit, is the fact that, in a weak jobs market, those with little or no choice will work harder to make up for those not doing much. In a nutshell, as a result, people in this kind of advantageous position have no interest in a radical and enduring improvement in the labour market. If it does pick up, the different parties would have to strike a new 'deal', probably leading to a shift in the division of labour. A number of comparative studies

have looked at differentials in the amount of time worked and productivity between tenured and temporary workers. There again, however, companies have 'embargoed' the findings, with no hope of the
embargo being lifted.

This raises the question of the strategies organizations adopt when
they feel the need to do better, indeed to do 'better with less', in order
to address these new demands. All of the strategies I have had occasion to observe, and which I will be presenting in what follows, point
to a reduction in the organization's reliance on human labour, since
they see it as unreliable, haphazard, uncontrollable and thus, when
the pressure of events builds up, an object that is not to be trusted.

One way of going about this is to 're-Taylorize' the work so that
its pace no longer depends on the person performing it or on his
goodwill, but on a more or less objective collective norm, one that
in any case reflects the needs of the firm. That is just what Taylor,
Fayolle and their followers wanted, namely to reassert control over
work and to make the pace of work independent of the individual
performing it.

Another way is to push 'automation' to its limits, obeying a logic in
which using the possibilities of technology to the full becomes an
end in itself, coterminous with 'progress'. France is a 'world cham-
pion' of automation. Its dream is a 'fully automated metro' system
and cashier-free supermarket checkout counters. Who cares if the
barcode can't smile? But one would have to be terribly blinkered to
imagine that 'that's just the way things are'. Other countries approach
things very differently (e.g., the USA, contrary to a common miscon-
ception in France), using technology 'as and when needed' and not as
a providential substitute for human labour when it falls out of favour.

Employment and work: two sides of the same coin

Another alternative is to delocalize. But public opinion frowns on its
perceived indifference to 'economic patriotism' and indeed patriotism
tout court, where keeping jobs on home soil is a matter of elementary
civic virtue. This accounts for the episodic fascination with certain
manufacturing activities, owing to the high profile and dramatic
conflicts they have sparked in the early years of this century, but also
because their demise modifies the everyday surroundings in which

we have grown up. Regardless of our religion, few among us would fail to experience some nostalgia were churches to vanish from our towns and villages. Yet only a handful of economists bother to take seriously the importance of manual labour in the car industry's 'value chain'.

And yet we need to re-establish here the reality of the different factors at work: I noted above that under-working was as much the outcome of lax oversight by managers as of 'laziness' on the part of those actually doing the work. I am now obliged to note that delo-calizations are intended as much to move to where labour is cheaper as to where the labour is, *tout court*. Once again, this is a 'systemic' collective responsibility, to use the sociologist's jargon.[3] More gen-erally, it is hard to avoid observing that these counterproductive practices – on both sides – are conspiring to 'kill' tomorrow's jobs. In other words, I am talking not just about work today but also about work tomorrow, observing that work and employment are – only in part – the two facets of a single history. And that in turn is helping to dismantle the intergenerational solidarity so sorely beset on other fronts as well.[4]

One last point on this subject: in the popular imagination, under-working is largely a civil service attribute, or at least in those parts of the civil service we can mock without risk. After all, no one would claim that nurses could possibly be under-worked: we might need them to care for us at some stage, so the thought that they might display less than unstinting devotion is intolerable. Yet my studies of the healthcare sector show that poor hospital organization and rigid procedures lead to severe overload in some units, while others are notoriously under-worked, with ample resources ... except where the patient is! Although the foregoing is something our societies cannot bring themselves to face up to, the rules that govern how hospitals function apply to all other organizations as well: the hospital is a complex and diverse reality that cannot be boiled down to a handful of ideological or partisan clichés, ranging from 'idle bureaucrats' to ritual complaints of 'under-resourcing'.

Even so, the phenomenon is surely more widespread in the civil service and kindred organizations, such as state-owned and formerly state-owned corporations. This is a reflection of what everyone knows: that government has always been a soft touch as an employer, since it has the resources to cave in to pressure from its employees, sometimes giving in even before the pressure builds up. Let the finger become caught up in this spiral of giving in, and very soon it's the hand and then the arm. But this is a partial approach, in both senses of the word. This is because under-working also occurs in the market sector, mostly in diffuse and in different, less 'tolerated' forms, though we all know what they involve: endless meetings that seem to go nowhere, lengthy breaks and all of the ways people have found to deal with today's increasingly harsh working conditions. There is always a way to duck out from under the pressure of work, if only for a moment.[5] I will come back to this theme later on.

This brings me to a case that goes well beyond what I have just been discussing, taken from the market sector.[6]

This concerned the agrifood or agribusiness sector, and the firm in question was part of a larger group. Its task was to prepare orders of widely varying sizes daily and then to deliver them, generally directly to retailers. Two observations struck me as a result of my interviews:

- First, that this was an environment that had 'lost its norms' as far as the criteria of what is normal and what is not regarding work and the management of human resources were concerned. These norms had unravelled with the passage of time. Obviously, this was not something anyone wanted, wished for or planned. It simply occurred gradually, as a result of a tacit and implicit arrangement between management, which wanted its products delivered on time (some were perishable) and for which labour productivity was of marginal importance, and a union that had gradually come to be dominant and was by now hegemonic. This union grasped the importance of what it 'controlled', namely an 'uncertainty' as sociologists would call it, and was determined to benefit from, and enable its followers to benefit from, this favourable situation. Nor should we forget the role played by the factory inspectors in the emergence of this environment, their rapid turnover no doubt preventing them from fully understanding the long-term consequences of their decisions.
- Second, a state of unrest existed, which on analysis turned out to be initially 'imaginary' and then strategic concerning the themes of the harshness of working conditions and the resulting violence, including among the employees themselves.

When fact is stranger than fiction

At the root of this twofold observation, our analysis shows that we are dealing here with a classic question of management's priorities, above and beyond its boilerplate talk of productivity and quality. This priority was that of a powerful player in its market, enjoying a positive reputation among its clients and concerned with ensuring that this was not harmed by labour disputes, which could damage relations with these clients. 'Delivering' the goods in the right conditions always took priority over any other consideration, especially since an earlier strike had shown the damage that labour unrest could do.

This concern with customer satisfaction 'at all costs' led the firm to give ground on work 'discipline' in a succession of retreats. These retreats had increasingly become unavoidable as part of the workforce came to see how they could profit from this situation in terms of the expected work rate, absenteeism and generally rejecting any kind of constraint in a setting that already imposed few such constraints.

The situation steadily deteriorated over time, as supervisors and foremen looked on. Very soon they too grasped the real 'rules' in this environment. Under-working came to be an accepted norm, prompting some sharp reactions and descriptions on the part of a handful of actors, speaking confidentially. A selection of their comments is given below:

'People here don't give a damn about leaving their work unfinished. They always think someone else will do it. And even the foremen don't always bother to turn up. There's a general sense of "I'm alright, Jack" that's taken hold.'

'I don't believe there's any discipline here anymore. Some things go pretty far with no one getting reprimanded. And when you see who's skiving off, it's always the same people, of course.'

'The ones under me [this is a foreman talking] *have been here 30 years. They get here in the morning and they dawdle, they have a coffee, do the crosswords. One's a shop steward; he just slopes off telling me "I'm off to the room"* [the shop stewards' room]. *I don't know where he's going. He goes off when he feels like it. It's terrifying!*

The plant is running slowly. And there's nothing I can say to them because it's taboo. If I say anything to them they'll take it the wrong way and turn it to their advantage, the way they always do.'

'People are off work systematically. It's unbelievable. And no one does anything about it. It's starting to make me sick.'

Leaving aside their endless descriptions of under-working and the unease it can instil in this section of the population, these first-person accounts point to one consequence of this situation, which had in turn, in terms of pure systemic logic, aggravated the positions of supervisors and foremen especially. As we can see, in the 'system' that was slowly emerging, the front-line supervisors were suffering the most.[7] They were squeezed between workers who could work only as much as they wished to and a 'management' – a term workers here used to designate executives in general – that was not on the shop floor, that always had an excuse to look the other way, to refuse to 'open a file' on the most flagrant cases and systematically refuse the sanctions called for by the front-line supervisors. This attitude triggered two reactions among the front-line supervisors, further accelerating the 'social breakdown' we have been charting:

- In the first case, supervisors 'leveraged' the remnants of power at their disposal, e.g., putting people up for promotion, naturally preferring the most reliable in their eyes. But in a climate as vitiated as this, these 'personalized' nominations, decided on strictly 'local' criteria (i.e., the nominee's personal relationship with the foreman and his personal opinion of that person's qualities), inevitably prompted accusations of 'favouritism' and a fierce denunciation of 'arbitrariness' on the part of these 'petty officials'. Here too, the lack of a handful of simple norms, as observed above, hindered the day-to-day management of personnel, ratcheting up the general climate of suspicion, frustration and indeed the feeling that it was not worth bothering to do any more. Sociologists call this a 'vicious circle'.
- To make matters worse here, this unit's troubled labour management practices were exacerbated by the fact that some workers received 14 months' pay while some received only 13 months' pay, the kind of gap that always creates problems in the workplace. And the system of individual bonuses just added to the overall picture.

Hardly surprisingly, when no one bothers with even a few basic rules in the workplace, the actors concerned also suspect a lack of rules in the way they are managed. Here there almost seems to be a 'collective effort' to degrade the world of work, in which 'managerial sloth' encouraged a climate of sloth all round.

- The second reaction (strategy) on the part of the front-line supervisor is a sense of bitterness and its practical expression, withdrawal symptoms, which in turn serve to amplify the anomic nature of this system. Indeed, these individuals made no secret of the fact, as is clear from the following excerpts:

> *'People stop half an hour before the end of the shift, and in any case there's nothing I can say, since no one would listen...'*

> *'Yes, people are afraid of everything! Fear of conflict, fear of the factory inspectors and all that means the superiors stay out of things, since no one's ever dared bare their teeth.'*

> *'There's been a heavy emphasis on dialogue and on the shop stewards. In fact, they've done away with order, and now there's a real problem of hierarchy. One gets the impression they've bought labour peace by giving people rights with nothing in return. And now it's up to us to make do with this...'*

To sum up, the 'trap' these front-line supervisors were caught in is plain to see: they truly believed in their work – their responsibilities – and all they could do was to take note of the phenomena of underworking, or indeed of non-work (for night shifts especially), they dealt with daily. If they tried to do something about it, relations quickly turned sour, exposing them to the hostility of a dominant union, with no support from management. Clearly, once again, the anomie in this environment is systemic.

In addition, the practices described above spread all the faster, in an atmosphere of relative indifference, when the actors concerned have little or no experience of any other workplace setting. There is no 'alternative norm' to offset the dominant norm. People in this environment have no means of comparison, so they are hard put to say what is abnormal about it. This is a feature common to all organizations where this kind of practice has taken root. In contrast, it accounts for the alarm felt by people arriving from outside, especially when they have been hired to 'set things straight'. A seasoned engineer who recently arrived at the firm had this to say:

> *'I'd never seen under-working and laziness on a scale like this! Nowhere! It isn't a case of a few isolated instances. Here, it's a national sport, along with absenteeism. Twenty-six per cent, I was told last month! Can you imagine? One feels completely at a loss. They tell you that's all in the past, it's history, and finally it's accepted that an unspecified number of people are there to be paid without working.'*

Temporary workers: an adjustment variable

So where is the 'adjustment variable' needed to perform the tasks day in, day out and to keep this environment going, which otherwise looks doomed, given what we have observed there? We have already pointed out that, given the company's margins and its favourable market position, labour productivity was not a central feature of the firm's policy vis-à-vis its personnel. In fact, that is something of a euphemism. Nevertheless, the practical limit to the system was the need to 'get its products out', night and day, in conditions acceptable to its clients. Given that the company was by no means in a monopoly situation, it had limited scope to externalize its 'operating costs'.

Yet it was not this imperative that served to 'regulate' the system's excesses. By tacit agreement between all those concerned – management and the union – an 'adjustment variable' had been found. Willingly or not, this was the role played by temporary workers. We need to pause for a moment to consider this phenomenon: first, because everyone concerned acknowledged and accepted it; and, second, because it aroused highly emotional reactions and moral judgements. This is not surprising, as we are nearing the limits of what a human group is able or willing to reveal about its practices, so contradictory are they in relation to its prevailing rhetoric – management and union alike.[8]

Indeed, how can one look on quietly while an under-privileged – less privileged than the others in any case – category of workers 'pays' with their work for the enviable, and in this case very well-protected, situation enjoyed by the tenured workers? In fact, this sort of mechanism is far more widespread than social niceties are willing to admit. It is the mechanical outcome of the granting of privileges to a population: in order to enjoy its benefits, costs are 'externalized' to another population not entitled to those privileges. This is a kind of 'internal externalization', as opposed to the kind that is shifted on to the client or the environment in general. This is the role 'auxiliaries' have played, and still play, in the French civil service. They always end up getting their tenure, only to be replaced by others, since there is no such thing as privilege without exclusion.

In the firm dealt with here, this accounted for the 'initiation rite' temporary workers had to undergo. For a while, their work rate far exceeded that of the tenured workers, even that of the best-disposed workers; after the end of their trial period, they were accepted into the ranks of the elect, being offered the long-awaited full contract. This was as crucial as the temporary worker himself, since the situation would rapidly become intolerable if it became too protracted; the actors concerned accepted it because they expected a positive outcome. For the tenured workers, meanwhile, it would be counterproductive if it could be shown that in fact the firm worked better with temporary workers than with tenured workers, as is the case with the French state-run education system. Thus, the stream needed to be fed continuously, since a drastic fall in the number of temporary workers would be certain to destabilize the system. Meanwhile, the temporary worker himself would wait patiently and with resignation for the end of this transitional period, doing everything asked of him. As one of them put it:

> *'As a temporary worker, I'd rather not ask for another assignment. I'm waiting for them to say it. I could be a quality controller, for example. But I think that, as a temporary worker, I don't have the right to ask for that. So I'm waiting...'*

Therefore, it came as no surprise that all of the actors acknowledged the phenomenon without batting an eyelid, just so long as this state of affairs stayed inside the firm. Indeed, the distinction between tenured and temporary workers, and the 'functional' role it played, was the subject on which interviewees were most willing to express themselves:

> *'Of course, we fight harder to get hold of the temporary workers than those that get hired because they* [the latter] *have difficulty accepting*

it when we say something to them. So we ask more from the temporary workers.'

'The temporary workers work harder than the others, it's a fact. If only just to get them back on the job. But if everyone did their job, we wouldn't have so many temporary workers.'

'The fact that temporary workers work harder than those that get hired isn't an impression, it's a fact. The day they leave, productivity nosedives.'

'Someone who's hired obviously doesn't work at the same rate, doesn't have the same output. Little by little, they tend to work fewer hours.'

One can see how, in an environment like this, work ends up becoming traumatic for some of the actors, not only for the foremen who, as we have seen, are the chief victims, but also for all those who, for one reason or another, are upset or troubled when disorder reaches this point. And, indeed, the trauma proved all the deeper when actors gained the impression, rightly or wrongly, that a trade union and its most active members were the chief beneficiaries of this situation. The battlelines were drawn more clearly in light of this observation, still further undermining (if that were possible) this community's already splintered cohesion. People's comments grew harsher and more uncompromising:

'There are some shop stewards who milk the system for all it's worth, they're the biggest slackers. If people in a room are with a shop steward, then it's even harder to get them back to work. And that's an understatement!'

'What really gets me here ... there's a phenomenon ... the non-unionized and the unionized workers. They're the acme of laziness; they don't give a damn; they're wankers. The breaks, the dope, all that...'

These interview excerpts are not here just to provoke or shock the reader. As has been shown elsewhere, they show that when a human environment has 'gone off-course' to this extent, it ends up breaking free from all control and gradually loses touch with reality. Things that would be simply ridiculous or obscene elsewhere now become possible. 'Deathly' would be one way to describe this 'possible world', since it not only reflects the abolition of any kind of norm as to what is acceptable and what is not, but it actually breeds opposition from within, among a disaffected fringe of the population. This disaffection stems from the fact that the organization has crossed – or is on the point of crossing – a limit where all of an organization's members share at least a common desire for its survival. And, indeed, when a manager says: 'For the trade unionists, it's the chaos that creates the jobs, and they tell me that they make a mess so as to make work for the cleaning company', it's clear that this is yet another step – a step too far? – in the destruction of the working community.

How to retain control by dramatizing the situation

But that is not the end of the story, for it can be a fascinating illustration of how a social system can 'snowball' out of control.

In the breakdown of this human community lurks the danger that some employees might drift away from the logic of the trade union and its environment. This was reflected in the revival of a trade union that used to be in the majority but which has now adopted a compensating strategy, speaking the language of responsibility and a return to order. To counteract this, it was imperative for employees that either belonged to or were close to the union currently 'running things' to whip up a sense of drama, in order to restore the minimum degree of consensus across the entire workforce. That should have sufficed to put management – whose extreme frailty we noted above – back on the spot. This explains the recurrence of the themes of working conditions (very poor) and violence (there were frequent outbreaks in the firm) on the company's labour relations agenda.

However, sociology has its 'techniques', one of which is to focus as much on what people do not talk about in an interview as on what they do talk about. The two themes mentioned in the previous paragraph never came up spontaneously in our interviews, in which a central question led interviewees to express themselves regarding the positive or negative aspects of their work. What they emphasized was the repetitive and boring aspects of their work, which they performed alone. They were surprised at the suggestion that the work might be physically demanding (a quick look at the shop floor is enough to see why), just as they grinned when questioned about possible stress linked to their activities. Once again, the issues that regularly and spontaneously recurred in interviews were injustice or the lack of a clear system of promotion or pay, along with the 'scandal of under-working'. Here are a few examples:

> *'Are there any problems with working conditions? No, I can't think of any. It isn't dangerous, it's safe. We try to avoid lifting heavy loads. As for stress... yes, ... I'd say yes for the temporary workers, because they come under the heaviest pressure. But that doesn't concern those who have been hired!'*

> *'It isn't hard work, no. Anyone who says the work's harsh here knows nothing of life. It really isn't a prison, here ... It's really cushy, here, you know!'*

> *'The temporary workers are stressed because they don't know whether or not they'll be hired. Apart from that, no, the work isn't stressful.'*

Thus, in this environment, the question of working conditions was a 'political' construct. However, it bore no relationship either to what could be seen with one's own eyes or above all to what the actors themselves felt, and the same was true for the question of violence. Questioned on this last point, a few people in the sample cited an incident – only one and always the same one – that did not even lead to a physical act. It involved two employees over an issue totally unrelated to work or life in the workplace. As to the rest, two interviewees, a manager and an operator, summed up the situation as follows:

> *'Violence? No, it was verbal, insults in the lifts. Sometimes they bring their outside problems into the workplace. But the conflicts have nothing to do with work, they're brought in from outside.'*

> *'I heard some talk about violence a while back, but it doesn't happen everyday! We're safe here.'*

On this question of violence, which everyone had heard about but no one has witnessed or suffered, the question deserves to be turned on its head: how come there weren't more outbreaks of violence among the actors in such a vitiated, unequal and occasionally anxiety-breeding environment? Part of the explanation for this lay in the rigorous social control exerted in this community. Everyone, even those harshest in their criticism of the system's breakdown, acknowledged this: they benefited, or had benefited, from the system's anomie. What we are seeing here is a de facto collective complicity, one that is hard for the individual to extricate himself from. In that sense, my interviews provided an outlet for some of the actors. Moreover, despite management's vacillations over pay policy and promotions, employees were not prepared to give them the benefit of the doubt. Both they and the front-line supervisors held management partly responsible for the current situation. Finally, the highly individual nature of the work organization, for operators at least, was not conducive to any involvement in the life of the work community. On the other hand, all this set the scene for a more active, more determined minority to take control of this environment by 'rewarding' each worker sufficiently to snuff out any form of protest, at the risk of going too far and endangering the organization's very survival.

By now, the reader can see how this tale is going to end, or at least what comes next. Management had 'let slip' its control over its workforce to the point where a return to a more 'normal' situation by authoritarian means looked unlikely. On the other hand, it might be tempted to relieve the pressure and increase its 'autonomy' vis-à-vis a factor over which it had long since abandoned control. There were two possibilities, for example, which it had begun to explore at the time of the study. One was to intensify the computerization of its order preparation process – there was no major technological obstacle to this. The other was to bring back the assembly line, which would allow management to dictate the operator's work rate and not the reverse. In that event, there would be no alternative to observing that the present under-working (once again, this is systemic in the sense of being the outcome of interactions between the actors involved) had killed off tomorrow's jobs.

What is apparent in this case is the collective construction of an environment of work for which we then seek to ascribe responsibility to one of the actors. This served to jettison the simplistic notion that someone 'decided' and that that is simply how things were, or that some 'hidden hand' was able to manipulate people to arrive at this result. If that were true, all that would be needed would be to wait for a more 'courageous' person – that much-vaunted 'fresh blood' – to take things in hand and restore order. Things were different in reality and bore little relation to the vain quest for a 'leader' who would come and take charge. What I have observed is that in an environment as 'constructed' as this, in which all of the actors (management included) benefit from the existing situation, change can only come from a variation in a component of the environment. To put it another way, organizations only very rarely challenge their endogenous nature. That is why governments or states rarely reform themselves, except when a particularly violent crisis damages their credibility among potential lenders. And even then, in the case of businesses, the 'time for change' generally arrives as a result of the emergence of a 'newcomer' to the market or a sudden drop in profit margins that irks a hitherto quiescent shareholder. In other words, as I have explained elsewhere, change comes not when it is necessary, but when it is possible.[9]

*

One could object that the case described above is a very special one, an outlier only partially reflecting reality. In that case, here is another one, drawn from a radically different sector and concerning a major manufacturer in southern Europe.[10] Once again, here we will be able to observe these practices of everyday under-working, and above all the difficulty of 'reasserting a grip' on this type of situation, even via a policy of cautious, patient, small incremental steps. It will also be seen that for this company, unlike the previous one studied, the French state was for a long time its main shareholder, a logical outcome of the 'civil war' France experienced in the last century.

As such, the 'system' formed by this company (it had only a single location) functioned well, even if it did so at a particularly high cost in the form of acceptance of under-working as the dominant norm and of its natural consequence – withdrawal on the part of the supervisors – when they were not cast into the camp of the operatives. Needless to say, if it ever became necessary to cope with the demands of the marketplace, this mode of operation would pose real problems in terms of labour productivity, an issue that had yet to be dealt with. The situation, as it appeared at the time of the study, was reminiscent of the situation of the car maker Renault before the arrival of Georges Besse: publicly, the firm's priority was quality and production costs, while in reality labour relations were the prime focus of attention. The predominant concern was the 'fear of labour unrest', and this underlay every important decision; paradoxically, this stood in the way of listening to the firm's employees. Relations with the trade unions were institutionalized, which acted as a proxy for the relationship with the entire workforce. In other words, the trade union enjoyed a monopoly situation in the employees' market and saw no reason not to take advantage of the situation.

Taking what the actors had to say at face value gave a pretty good clue as to the prevailing climate and practices on the shop floor. As in the previous case, 'deleterious' was the first adjective that sprang to mind for the outside observer. Here is how a shift foreman (a front-line supervisor) described the operators' day:

> 'They start at 6.30. Until 7.00 or 7.15, I keep my mouth shut. In any case, if I say something to them, they'll take an hour and a half to adjust the machine, where I know it should take 20 minutes, and after that they'll go off to see the doctor. At 8.30, those that stay behind take a meal break. And sometimes, they'll down tools an hour or even an hour and a half before the end of the shift to clean up.'

A manager made the same observation:

> 'There is a real problem of absenteeism. Some people simply say: "I'm not coming in." There are even some who don't give any warning at all. So it's me that has to call them.'

Operatives themselves, once they felt confident, saw things in much the same way. As one of them put it:

> 'There are people who say it's Club Med here. And there are a lot of people around me who say I'm in a holiday camp. It is true we have a lot of advantages here, and I'm not oppressed by the work, really not.'

Going into detail for a moment, the laxity was visible in the work itself and its particularly languid pace, interrupted by countless discussions and asides. Confronted with this, the executives were forced to make do with whatever came to hand, as described unenthusiastically by one of them:

> 'I have a technique for breaking up discussions, I become involved myself, and that way I break up the group.'

Making difficulties for the front-line managers

One cannot help wondering why managers and supervisors (shift foremen and unit managers, for example) responded so limply to this situation, even at the risk of finding themselves in the position of the 'adjustment variable' in an emergency. An initial reason for this lay in the firm's HR practices, to which we will return later, so illustrative were they of some of contemporary management's shortcomings. For the moment, it is sufficient to observe the vicious circle engendered by this company's large-scale recourse to subcontracting. We will then be able to put our finger on the systemic nature of collective life in the workplace, as in other institutions.

The company responded to the very rapid growth in its market and constraints relating to its industrial capacity of facilities by regularly stepping up its use of subcontractors. Management justified this on the grounds that it provided flexibility and a means of cutting costs, given the firm's internal rigidity. The other, unanticipated, side of the coin was that the managers and supervisors had gradually lost their grip on both time and flows, being conditioned by the performance of organizations by now totally out of their control. The problem was exacerbated by the fact that suppliers, as nearly always happens in cases like this, had skilfully exploited the extreme segmentation between the firm's different departments, e.g., buyers, logistics, production and maintenance. In a word, the supplier now acted as the 'integrator' of these departments, which no longer had any contact with each other; moreover, their segmentation consistently served as an excellent excuse for not doing things as provided for in the initial contract or on time.

To cope with the situation, front-line managers had had to demand greater internal flexibility, but to obtain this they had been forced to negotiate a kind of 'you scratch my back, I'll scratch yours' relationship. As a result, supervisors had managed to persuade operators to work Saturdays, and sometimes even Sundays, in return for an implicit undertaking to say nothing about the pace of work. As a result, they let workers 'drink 10 coffees a day', 'we don't snoop on them', 'people can easily stretch out their meal breaks' and 'nothing is done to ensure working hours are respected'.

Front-line managers were consequently continually obliged to negotiate with operatives. Given that, in an organization still profoundly influenced by its tradition as a state-owned body, they wielded none of the traditional levers inherent in their function in terms of systems of pay and promotion, etc., and they took refuge in a system of managing labour relations individually in order to get everyone to show the necessary goodwill. This presumably explains why, in this environment, personal problems constantly crept into labour relations. Rarely, in all of the studies I have conducted, have I heard so much talk as in this firm of divorce, sickness and more generally all the miseries and misfortunes of life.

Not that this prevents general laxity and under-working from becoming an almost universally accepted norm, bearing a striking resemblance to what Simone Weil described in *La Condition Ouvrière* in the 1930s.[11] But here we are a far cry from 'infernal work rates'. This generally accepted norm of 'doing no more than the minimum' is reinforced, far more than counterbalanced, by the only 'counter-norm' present in the workplace, namely quality. The latter is brandished as a justification for slowing down the rate of work and for stoppages, and for any unduly visible violation of the supposed work rate. At the same time, everyone in the world of the operatives took care to ensure that no one breached the norm, and newcomers soon learnt what the rules were. An operative described it thus:

> *'Anyone who tries to go faster, speed things up, gets a dirty look. There are some people who make sure they're not around when we're machining parts, they run their machines empty.'*

A young supervisor made the same observation:

> *'We haven't taught people to do more than they're asked here, and in any case we don't try to. The foreman thinks it isn't his job. In fact, our job is trying to keep the workers happy. We don't want any trouble. That's the only real concern.'*

Stepping back a bit, we can observe the norm's construction, once again a systemic process: supervisors, undermined by the lack of any means of overseeing the operatives (and the tendency is gaining ground all the time), acquiesced in this minimalist norm or approach to work, and the group easily enforced it, especially since the organization's extreme segmentation effectively protected each of the actors from attempts to shift responsibility on to them.

Make no mistake: the message from management readily 'endorsed' and rationalized the situation. Hardly surprisingly, there was a vast gulf – reflecting their physical distance – between what senior management had to say, with its verbal modernism and modish notions, and the reality experienced by the actors on the ground, including the 'other' managers working on the shop floor. Where the upper echelons spoke of 'industrial excellence', the others merely saw things reaching the limits of what was reasonable. They inhabited different worlds and saw things differently. Above all, each group tried to protect itself in its own way, through substandard work for some and through rhetoric far removed from real life for others.

'The foremen aren't up to listening to people', said one operator, to which another added: 'Nowadays, they've added rungs to the ladder. Those at the top haven't a clue what's going on.' And a third concluded: 'Anyway, there's a wall now between the higher-ups and the workers. It's the unit supervisors who act as a buffer. They're the ones who are most isolated. The ones above them just go on saying "just get on with it"...'

What strikes one is that, leaving aside a small minority that benefited from the situation, no one seemed happy with it. None of the actors expressed the slightest enthusiasm, or indeed cynicism, about things, just a deep sense of resignation, a great deal of passiveness, and above all distrust of the other parties. As so often happens, the system here was caught in a never-ending lose-lose spiral: managers thought that there was nothing they could do, trapped between a base that had grown all-powerful thanks to the 'don't make waves' syndrome, and the operatives themselves, who could not understand why nothing was being done to break out of this rut. We were dealing here with an immature system, a system of non-confidence, which satisfied no one and bred despair in those most clearly aware of what was going on.

When the people from human resources complicate matters

To cap it all, it is worth noting that the human resources (HR) department's mode of operation and its policies served to 'consolidate' the system. This was so blatantly obvious that everyone concerned knew of this and deplored it, and that included the trade unions, even though they benefited from the situation. This was because, as in all bureaucratic organizations, the task of managing labour relations slowly grew apart from operations and came to be an activity in its own right, governed by its own logic, disconnected from the needs of those in charge of production – who suffered the practical consequences of decisions taken elsewhere. To put it another way, there seemed to be no clear realization in this firm that the way it evaluated, promoted and paid people was one of management's main 'levers'. But those who decided HR policy had no notion of the concept of the 'lever'.

At a very superficial level, it might be observed that nothing was done to take account of a particularly elderly population of employees mainly concerned with 'reap[ing] the maximum advantage before the end', to quote one interviewee. This population had grown passive and fatalistic over time and was naturally concerned with its short-term advantages, which were considerable, as we have seen. One could scarcely count on them to throw their support behind a logic shift. But, above all, the decisions, taken far from the shop floor, were governed by a logic that was either 'political' (in order to avoid any possible reaction on the shop floor) or 'moral' (equal treatment for all), though it is hard to see what that had to do with the demands of management. In this way, the firm was constantly trying to 'depersonalize' still further all of its dealings with individuals, regardless of their contribution to the performance (or under-performance) of the whole. What carried the day here was a purely administrative logic based on general, impersonal rules; however, in so doing, the firm went well beyond the demands and hopes of at least some of the unions. An experienced unionist wryly remarked to me:

> *'The centralized way our HR department works, with systematic raises every three years, harks back to the Stalinist era.'*

All of this functioned as a self-fulfilling prophecy. To cope with any eventuality, the firm had taken on board the norm it believed to be acceptable to the group, having itself defined it, i.e., 'indifferentiation' or treating everyone alike, thereby robbing line supervisors of possible means of action. As observed earlier, the latter had taken refuge in 'individual labour relations', i.e., dealing with difficult cases, the only area they could still call their own and around which they still enjoyed some room for manoeuvre. In other words, the roles had been reversed: the HR department adopted and amplified the logic of the unions – something the unions hadn't even asked for – while the supervisors withdrew into a state of apathy[12] at best, though in some cases 'accentuating' their behaviour instead, as has been observed elsewhere.[13] The most 'motivated' among them were reduced to finding peripheral margins for negotiation, such as whether or not to assign operators most in need of money to night shifts. And they were perfectly aware of this situation:

> 'To handle people, you first need to take account of everything that goes without saying, and that's quite a lot.'

> 'The HR department works with favoured partners. It's the trade unions that give HR a different view of the firm from ours.'

Even the operators condemned, or at least deplored, this situation:

> 'The slackers get just the same rewards as the rest. And in addition, I'm never asked what I think about the people who work with me. I don't think that's normal at all.'

One of the most distinctive features of firms that have 'let work slip' is their constant talk of 'industrial excellence', the pressures of international competition and so on; however, people see this as flatly contradicting the way they manage their human relations day to day. In other words, the climate will remain pernicious as long as the system for managing human resources in particular and management in general is inconsistent with the firm's stated ambitions, to the greater benefit of those wishing to profit from this situation. They respond to a system that has gone awry through deviant behaviour in their day-to-day work or by seeking to protect themselves. Sociologists in the 1970s, my predecessors, came up with very similar findings. This goes to show that when it comes to the way organizations really function, things probably change more slowly than we think, once we scratch beneath the surface and try to get a handle on the realities of everyday life. To confirm this, let's stay with this firm and take a look at the trade unions.

The dread of labour unrest

One common feature of 'bureaucratic' organizations is that the unions live and thrive on this 'dread of labour unrest'. This is not a cause but a consequence of the deviations described above. Two possible strategies flow from this: either they 'radicalize' their position – especially in periods of acute crisis, as sometimes occurs in the country concerned – widening their protest to issues beyond those strictly involving the firm itself; or they cast around for issues on which to stake their demands, wages, for example, that seem pretty far removed from usual practice in this part of Europe. But losing touch with reality in this way is not peculiar to the unions alone. As in the previous case study, it stemmed from the anomie of a system that had given up producing and defending behavioural norms in the workplace. It stemmed too from the 'pincers' formed by the prevailing apathy and bolstered by the centralized, bureaucratic nature of HR management at its 'core'. Just like the minority unions, some employees felt a little uneasy in this context: there was a vague aspiration for 'something else', which collided with the lack of any credible project. One does not have to be a Cassandra to argue that experience shows that this type of stalemate usually ends in crisis, with a heavy human and financial cost. At the same time, and this is not the least of the paradoxes, in the present case no one, not even among senior management, had any sense of 'economic' urgency. On the other hand, the routine malaise caused by this pernicious climate was very real.

I revisited this company a year later. Its top managers were impatient to learn whether their campaign of 'reconquest', waged with managerial techniques imported from the USA, had produced, or at had least begun to produce, any effects. The results came as a disappointment, since we again found the same features as before, and in some cases aggravated. Not that their efforts had been in vain; simply, one cannot seriously hope to shake up an environment as complex, rigid and entrenched as this in so short a timeframe, unless one is prepared to go through a major crisis, as we shall now see.

*

This large furniture firm had a large plant in northern France.[14] A dispute broke out there that lasted for nearly two weeks, to everyone's surprise, and left lasting scars. It came as a surprise because, as everyone admitted, 'no one saw it coming', neither top management nor the local managers, nor even the strikers themselves, including those who proved to be the most determined. The very idea that a union could have foreseen, controlled and organized everything does not stand up to scrutiny. We will come back to this. The surprise no doubt explained the turn taken by the dispute, its chaotic aspect, the interminable interlude between its onset and the initial formulation of explicit – and unrealistic – demands, as well as the frustration that marked its ending.

Big company logic, local logic

However, that this state of affairs should have come as a surprise was itself amazing, given that all those involved interpreted the origins of this sudden burst of unrest in roughly the same way. Still more surprising was that it was hard to distinguish between strikers' and non-strikers' views of what caused the strike. What drove them to behave so differently was far more likely their personal financial situation, i.e., whether or not they could afford to lose an indeterminate portion of their thirteenth month's wages, than any divergence in their assessment of the situation.

This was a protracted strike. It was a bitter one too, and both these features could no doubt be put down to the lack of a 'culture of labour disputes' at this site. But how was it that in the final ballot, which brought the conflict to an end after two weeks, nearly two-thirds of the personnel voted to prolong the strike,[15] as if sensing they would never have another opportunity to express the full extent of their resentment and anxiety? Even today, there subsists a lingering atmosphere verging on loathing between strikers and non-strikers. Therefore, we need to penetrate the everyday life of this plant in order to understand just how disruptive a brutal attempt to reassert control over the situation can prove, bearing in mind that no one imagined it could last so long.

Generally, there were two opposing logics within this firm, and they crystallized here, at this 'historical' plant dating back to the company's founder. There was the logic of the firm as a whole, now a group of companies doing business nationwide and also internationally for a handful of specialized products. We are dealing with a 'globalized' world here.

The local logic was very different. This grew out of an early twentieth-century provincial paternalism typical of this part of France. There is a long tradition in northern France of an explicit alliance between a firm's founder and its personnel, with the successful founder abundantly sharing the fruits of his success with his employees. Speaking of this firm's founder, whom he had known well, an old trade unionist deeply committed to the labour movement volunteered: 'If all the bosses were like that, we wouldn't need unions.' Thus, one needs to grasp how this 'old system' worked, since it was this that was brutally – savagely, according to those involved – turned upside down by the new management that took control after the classic 'crisis of governance' that ensued after the death of the pioneer, mourned by all of course.

Our analysis showed that this system featured three forms of 'regulation': distributive regulation, managerial regulation and social regulation, which ensured a high degree of stability, if not economic efficiency. These no longer existed under the battering ram of the 'professional' managers, but they had not been replaced by other integrating mechanisms, and it was this, as one could imagine, that triggered the crisis.

Therefore, there was a process of regulation via an abundance of means, both human and financial. Even those who went on strike for more pay willingly admitted that 'people were well-treated in this firm'. There is no point insisting that, where human means are concerned, the system never functioned with precision, either in the past or now, and that we were probably not far removed from the 'under-working' practices observed earlier. The difference here is that these practices grew up by 'mutual consent', allowing front-line supervisors to deal with human problems despotically in appearance, though with considerable benevolence in reality. This can be useful when personal, family and working relationships are closely interwoven.

Managerial regulation functioned via 'complaints channels' that dispensed justice and fairness, which are essential conditions for preserving harmony in an environment where everyone knows everyone else. Under the old system, the body formed by the shop stewards, managers, the HR department and one or other of the founding family members gave everyone a feeling that they had a channel through which they could seek redress at any time. This was replaced in this plant by a management that was felt to be particularly 'tough', having done away with the possibility of 'referring the matter up', which fuelled a genuine sense among the workforce of having been abandoned. For example, though this may seem unimportant, everyone noticed that no member of senior management now lived at the company's birthplace. Indeed, when asked about the dispute, these managers invariably began their reply with: 'I've heard it said…' This was a new method of management, presumably management by hearsay.

Finally, there was the social regulation mechanism, which was probably the most important. Thanks to its flexibility and to various arrangements, but also and above all thanks to the aforementioned abundance of means, this system served to manage all those human micro-conflicts inherent to this type of environment. This is a crucial aspect, since making all those daily human adjustments so essential to life in any community is a subtle affair, one that demands detailed knowledge of the population concerned, which constitutes a long learning process; it also demands the financial and human resources needed to direct resources flexibly to the right place. The new managers tried to form new work teams on a 'co-optation' basis – an intellectually appealing idea, but disastrous in practice! Not only did it mean that some people were excluded – they were politely transferred to a 'support team' – but above all it destroyed the traditional mechanisms for making day-to-day adjustments. It placed quasi-supervisory responsibilities on the shoulders of operatives, who coexisted alongside the others solely thanks to mediation by a third party, the frontline manager. To put it in trivial terms, this reorganization 'messed up' the existing human system, undermining the subtle equilibriums forged over time, and in doing so undermined the actors themselves. At the time of the strike, this pretty brutal assault on the traditional forms of regulation forged a series of 'unholy alliances', which we will describe below. Locally, as one manager put it, people felt management had applied the 'logic of rape'. It is worth noting that this term is as violent as those used in the preceding cases, even though the working environment here was a politer one, in appearance at least.

As we have seen, added to this was the fact that senior management was now geographically distant, creating a sense of anxiety given that the founding father used to live locally. One can readily understand the feeling gradually rising to the surface: that business was going badly (this sector of the furniture industry had been hard hit by the recent economic and financial crisis) and that the site had been left to its own devices by this absentee management – which in any case seemed more preoccupied by its own internal squabbles than by the need to deal with the real problems. This comment is not without interest and is reminiscent of the situation at Air France when it 'blew up' at the end of 1993. Here too, with a few exceptions, there was no major opposition to the entry of the plant, and of the company as a whole, into the world as it is. Here lies the difference compared to what we observed earlier. On the other hand, there was real concern as to this management's capacity to execute this transformation on acceptable terms, given that it had 'disappeared' and was unfamiliar with local ways and realities. Here is what a young operator had to say:

> *'The oldies don't understand that the world has changed. There was a golden age when the profits were shared out more fairly. It's hard for them. I can understand. But there's got to be something for everyone. And on that score one can do a lot better than they're doing right now.'*

In these circumstances, as often happens, outside events in the economy served to crystallize people's fears and set the scene for a series of 'unholy' alliances: for example, across-the-board pay cuts (through the elimination of bonuses and incentive pay) in the two years prior to the dispute gave employees with divergent interests a reason to 'go on strike together'. The oldest workers, with little to lose in the long run but a lot to lose in the short run, took a radical line. This gave them an opportunity to vent their frustrations over an abortive early retirement plan. As they put it, they went on strike 'for the younger ones', so their jobs would not come under threat and to enable them to earn a decent wage.

These people knew their best years were behind them, but they felt a huge sense of injustice at the way in which this transformation had been treated. The explanation given to them – that it was vital to reassure the new shareholder – was a heavy blow, feeling as they did that they were the first to deserve reassurance, especially when management in Paris told them that having a bonus was a 'privilege'!

Similarly, this clumsy approach to questions of pay brought together two groups that had hitherto ignored and consequently distrusted each other, and that had formerly envied each other, on the strength of second-hand tittle-tattle no one had ever bothered to verify. The 'makers' and the 'logistics crowd' (the plant's two main activities) were united by the same fears, and money matters kindled the fire by giving concrete substance to their deep-seated if diffuse anxieties.

The importance of anticipating the effects of change

This explains why the strike was sudden and spontaneous. 'We came out, and we didn't go back in', says an operator. Nobody controlled it: each day was felt to be a new adventure, affording an opportunity to discover or rediscover 'lost solidarities'. From one point of view, the human warmth of the strike recalled the protective world of the past. But it unravelled too, as the interests of the different actors diverged. Some categories, such as the foremen, began to feel genuinely uneasy. Others realized they had been caught up in a dispute they didn't feel was theirs, while the most radical (who were also the best educated) began talking of a wider fight against capitalist society. This shows how hard it is to set about changing a working environment when it is too comfortable. And the conclusion the cases presented in this chapter point to is that the greater the 'acquired rights' and the more their beneficiaries are disconnected from the realities 'of a world' they cannot (or would rather not) visualize changing, the more difficult it is. In that respect, the endogamous nature of recruitment that is a feature of these firms (people work there from father to son) makes them even more 'hermetic'. Consequently, 'common sense' messages founded in necessity, delivered by managers trained in abstract reasoning, gain little traction. All too often, common sense makes no sense.

It is not enough to explain to employees that the changes are necessitated by market developments or pressure from customers. Markets and customers are exogenous factors. When they do impact on the organization and its processes, there is a disconnect between an intellectual understanding of them and a practical apprehension of the results of action being taken. Even if opinion polls show that 'the majority of employees understand that...', these same employees will react on the basis of the practical consequences of the changes in their daily lives. Questions asked in companies concerning 'support for...' or even of 'meaning' are too abstract: an actor can support or agree with a necessity yet still reject its consequences. To see this as contradictory is to think in terms of formal logic, not in terms of understanding of human reality.

Indeed, that is why communications policies soon reach their limits. Explaining necessity is certainly necessary, but it really isn't sufficient. The real question, the concrete question, is about anticipation or foresight: foreseeing the real effects of changes on the daily lives of actors, on the way they work (or don't work!), muddle through, deal with their problems and manage relationships for a start; in addition, on the way they foresee how people are likely to react to the changes one is about to impose on them in the name of market exigencies. The question, then, is not how to convince people willingly to accept what is about to happen, it is to hammer out a 'new deal' with the employees, one very different from the traditional forms of protection in the workplace, but one that makes the transformations acceptable to those involved. This need to come up with a win-win situation between the changing company and its employees offers a fruitful line of investigation.

2
Silo Organizations and their Unwanted Side-Effects

Criticizing work in silos, in 'organ pipes', is as commonplace as noting the persistence and spread of this mode of organization. There is a simple reason for this, which we will discuss later in this chapter, namely that this way of doing things was originally introduced as a 'scientific mode of the organization of work' (Taylor, Fayolle). It served to define clear tasks that could be performed in a predictable manner by individuals, each of them interchangeable. As stated in the previous chapter, this reduces the dependence on human unpredictability to a minimum. Deviance is neither acceptable nor tolerated, since it would be seen as an expression of disagreement with 'science', which would in turn be either morally perverse or a sign of psychological disturbance. Yet that was regarded as the basis of mass production.

Side by side with the scientific critique of Taylorism, which argues, among other things, with Taylorism's assumptions as to what people seek in their work, a 'humanist' critique of Taylorism has emerged. The vertical organization of work, it claims, robs the operative of an overall vision and hence of the possibility of grasping the 'whole', of which he produces only a part. This view holds that the logic of fragmentation and dispossession makes it all the harder to 'motivate' the operative and make him an active, involved actor in the process. This gave rise, in the 1970s, to the introduction of 'autonomous groups' and all those forms of work designed to lift the worker out of his condition as a 'human machine', at last giving him a chance to appropriate the 'reconstituted' results of his activity.

I have no hesitation in saying that this critique was intellectual and external to work *per se*. This is because, if there is one thing that is blindingly obvious in the early years of this century, it is the highly protective virtue of this 'silo' organization. To understand this, one needs to jettison the notion of 'silo' and grasp that of 'segmented and sequential' work. This says that not only do the tasks to be performed and their segmentation constitute the foundation of the organization of work, but also that these tasks need to be performed one after the other – that performance of the second presupposes completion of the first task. In the car industry in the 1980s, the process of 'designing', and hence defining, a product was entrusted to a firm's engineers. This meant that they were in charge of defining the manufacturing methods and processes. Needless to say, one cannot define the process without knowing the product, hence the unquestionable need for a succession of tasks and arranging them in a sequence.

The protection afforded by segmented, sequential work

What became clear, however, once the market started opening up (in response to an exogenous constraint), and once clients had the choice, is that there were two drawbacks to this form of organization, namely low quality at a high cost (people have referred to the 'additional cost of poor service' to describe the service provided by the civil service, the last bastion of Taylorism in its purest form). In the car industry, poor quality came to light through modifications leading to cost overruns. This brings us back to the notion of 'externalities', as long as these overruns could be passed on to the client, who had no alternative but to deal with them. Perverse? Not a bit of it: merely the strategic application of the highly protective virtues of work in its segmented, sequential form. In a word, we find here that instead of being a kind of mutilation, Taylorism acts as a protection.

This notion of work as a means of 'protection' has already been the subject of much discussion. Briefly, work is supposed to protect against the vicissitudes of life. This led to the emergence of the open-ended employment contract and 'statutes', which in France and Japan, for instance, set the scene for jobs for life. When the labour market suffers long-term deterioration, this feature of the employer/employee relationship comes to be paramount for employees, whereas employers see it as an obstacle to the flexibility they need.

Work in its segmented and sequential form protects the different members of the organization differently. To begin with, none of them is answerable for the result to the client, who is buffeted between the different parties, each assuring him that the mistake was made elsewhere and leaving him no opportunity to unravel the tangle facing him. We have all experienced the impenetrable maze through which 'files' meander from desk to desk, from one department to another, with no possibility of identifying who does what and who is 'accountable' for what eventually happens or how the result was reached. All this is not without consequences! One would have to be very naïve, or blind, not to see that the more competitors there are in a market, the greater the client's room for choice when confronted with a 'problem', thanks to his greater ability to exert pressure on his supplier. So we are indeed talking about protection from the client: the person who, in management rhetoric, is supposed to stand 'at the heart of the organization'; more prosaically, the organization's members are more concerned with keeping him on the sidelines. This is because, faced with the apparently contradictory demands of the customer with a vast choice before him ('give me more for less'), the organization of work is the obvious adjustment variable. Put simply, it means abandoning the segmented-sequential pair in favour of a different tandem: simultaneity-cooperative. This will progressively reduce the capacity for externalization, and the workplace will de facto become more 'confrontational'. I will return to this later on.

But that is not all! We have still not reached the heart of the matter. For this form of work affords another form of protection that proves in practice to be the most invaluable of all, in particular for managers. Protected as they are by the watertight walls of their silos and by the mechanics of the succession of tasks, they have no need to 'cooperate' with others, with their colleagues or with neighbouring departments. This notion of cooperation is interesting because of its highly positive connotations in our mental universe. A person who cooperates is someone who is open to others, who has nothing to hide and who willingly 'comes out into the open' for the benefit of the final result – here for the customer – but also for the greater good. But in fact, this is not so! This is yet another manifestation of the quasi-ideological dimension of corporate speak produced daily

by business schools and major consulting firms in their bid to refor-
mulate in acceptable terms the new constraints that organizations –
themselves under pressure – impose on their members.

Cooperation is not a natural or spontaneous form of behaviour,
at least not in everyday work settings. For the actors concerned, it
replaces autonomy with dependence, neutral relationships with
confrontation. This is precisely what administrative organizations,
to confine ourselves to their case only, have sought to avoid at all
costs. It helps us to understand their fierce resistance to switching
to a different way of working, for this would suddenly 'rob them'
of their protection, from users now turned into clients, from their
peers who now become colleagues. In a word, they have no wish
to be confronted with Jean-Paul Sartre's vision of 'hell', i.e., other
people.

Even if the possibilities of avoiding this were far fewer, the temptation
has always been just as great in the market sector. It is because cooperation is not natural behaviour that it was necessary to create it, to impose
it. The fact that companies have chosen to do so – introducing ever
more numerous and ever more complex 'processes' – has left us with a
cure that is worse than the disease.[1]

I take as my first illustration of this the case of an insurance company highly specialized in high value-added products.[2] We will focus
on a particular department, the one that measured the risks salespeople were about to take on. This is a complex task, since the profits
the company earned on these very special products could make it
expedient to turn a blind eye to transactions that could later prove
imprudent, in spite of the strict rules defining what could be done
and what could not, and the fact that these rules were known to all.
Indeed, everyone signed up to them, which is why the 'compliance'
department was so named – even in French.

At first sight, this department, as we will now call it, was an
organization with no particular problems. The vast majority of those
interviewed expressed no special concerns, sometimes even convey-
ing the impression of a featureless environment in which everyone
got on with their work in a routine fashion, with little room for
enthusiasm. Better still, the younger people there – and there were
a lot of them – said they were very happy to be there. They stressed
that the department was a very good place to learn and that a spell
with this part of the company was an excellent stepping-stone for

the rest of their career. In fact, many were contemplating continuing their career there.

The opaque universe of self-contained worlds

Yet, at the same time, after scratching beneath the surface, a highly 'technical', relatively opaque world emerged. Specialized insurance is inherently complex, less so in its organization than in the material it deals with, and it would be naïve to suppose otherwise. This explains why it was not possible to 'know everything' and consequently why what 'the others', here the other departments, were doing sometimes looked remote, if not to say obscure. What stood out above all was that, again by its nature, the department functioned in a hostile environment. The dominant model in the company was that of the 'salesman'. He was a highly specialized technician, the person actually in the marketplace, and so could reap large rewards for the community (and for himself too!) depending on the risks he was prepared to take. From then on, everything became clear: the department was the 'thorn in everyone's side'. To work in this department was to depend on those dealing directly with the clients, on those who brought in the cash and who therefore expanded the amount of variable compensation available. One can see why, in order to be successful, the work of the department called for a great deal of tact, failing which what might start out as a trial of strength entered into unthinkingly could turn into a rout for the unwary. The actors described the situation very well:

> *'Normally, they are required to consult us before embarking on this type of deal. But very often they don't do so, especially those that come from elsewhere* [from another company].*'*

> *'In a conflict with a salesperson, the golden rule is never to make things worse. Otherwise, the salesperson refers the matter to his superiors instead of answering my question. In which case they'll tell me I'm not being proactive and that I'm standing in the way of business. No, I prefer to smooth things over. You have to put the question to the salesperson so as not ruffle feathers. That's how it is...'*

As we can see, this was a job where those responsible for exercising 'control' could fairly easily 'get round the rules'. They came under significant pressure, and the scales between them and the people in sales were heavily tipped in favour of the latter. In other words, there was an 'implicit hierarchy' within this world of specialist insurance that did not favour the department – far from it. This explained why it had never been a priority area for IT investment, which had merely exacerbated its difficulties vis-à-vis those it dealt with. Employees complained bitterly about this and pointed to it as the main source of their difficulties.

On closer scrutiny, though, it looked as if the true cause of the department's problem lay elsewhere: a state of dependency like this *ought* to have implied a high degree of solidarity inside the organization. It *ought* to have bred homogeneity and cooperation among its members in order to offer those who it dealt with outside no room for manoeuvre. Yet the reverse was the case. In the current situation, the department was a fragmented organization, opaque even to those who worked for it, where information flowed poorly. To take a sociological image, it functioned like a honeycomb, being segmented and compartmentalized, where nobody knew what anyone else was doing, with much effort being duplicated as a result. Let's try to dig deeper.

'Who is responsible for what?', asked one member of the department when I asked him to describe its composition. Given that the department was extremely compartmentalized, not only did people not know each other, they didn't know what the others in the department were doing. An unmistakable sign was that when asked which working environment they belonged to or which was their centre of reference, people cited their unit inside the department, not the department itself. The actors themselves made much of this mutual ignorance, even though ultimately they had no clear perception of its consequences:

> 'Maybe Unit X works better than mine. I've no idea. I don't know them. In addition, there's a Chief Administrative Officer, though I don't really understand what he does. And then, people use incomprehensible jargon in this organization, and everyone pretends to understand each other tacitly.'

> 'Although there's quite a lot of communication inside my unit, I don't know everything that goes on in the department. In fact, my activity doesn't deal with the department's other activities. I don't work with the other units.'

'A person working in my unit doesn't feel part of the department. In fact, my unit is a state within a state: we don't know what the others are up to. That may be a problem, because there could be important connections with what the others are doing. We could be given advance warning. When you think about it, that's definitely a weakness.'

These were well and truly 'self-contained worlds', even if these segmentations faithfully replicated the company's business lines. Thus, it wasn't the structure that was the problem, but the way the organization worked in practice. The lack of cooperation and mutual ignorance prevented the department from capitalizing on information and knowledge. As a result, the different actors were unable to reap any benefit from the fact that, between them, they covered all of the company's activities, when dealing with outsiders focused on their 'business', with a short-term perspective on performance. This was something illustrated by this interview excerpt:

'The department's weakness is the lack of communication. It's hard to know where the entry point is. In fact there are too many. For any given subject, you have to talk to ten people. That's a lot, and there ought to be fewer. But that comes from the fact that, for many projects, there's no designated contact person.'

Let's pause for a moment to examine the consequences of this way of doing things. Needless to say, as we have seen, compartmentalization had many advantages for the organization's members. It protected them insofar as it let each person 'do their own thing', pursuing their own 'one-dimensional' logic without having to confront that of others. Moreover, no one was directly responsible for major difficulties when they arose. For those who wanted to – or for those who had just given up – it let them idle away their time. As one interviewee noted: 'Eighty per cent of people in the company have no obligation to produce results. They're very easily satisfied with average performance.'

But over and beyond this recurring aspect of life in organizations, which highlights their protective function, we saw nothing short of an 'administrative bureaucracy' in place of the 'dynamic management' that was a constant theme in the company's messages about itself. As a result, budgetary procedures (i.e., the allocation of resources) became disconnected from real needs, with no possibility of adapting means to the expanding workload, even though this affected different units to differing degrees. The same gestures were repeated over and over, and breaking the mould demanded tenacity and courage, with no guarantee of success. An old hand in the department echoed this view:

> '*Sometimes you find the doors are padlocked. People get stuck in a rut. It's vital not to get discouraged. You need to start all over again, because in any case, people here don't learn from their past mistakes.*'

What is more, the compartmentalization here was both horizontal (as we have just seen) and vertical, owing to the impressive number of management layers. This piling up of layers made the department less comprehensible not only to its members but also to outsiders dealing with it. In addition, it made the proper control of risk assessment and the conditions in which risks were assessed unreliable. One interviewee described the situation very accurately:

> '*There are far too many management layers: an analyst sees a file, then it is reviewed, then reviewed again … That breeds frustration for these analysts. The result is accumulated delays and poor quality vis-à-vis the salespeople.*'

Worse still, since the 'spontaneous' workings of this organization prevented it from responding to the demands of its 'clients' – even if they were internal clients – a whole array of networks served to overcome this shortcoming. This gave the actors a feeling, expressed many times over in interviews, of being in a highly 'political' environment with a strong measure of inequality of opportunity for the different actors to function in it effectively. The syndrome of the 'unequal society' predominated, which people found especially hard to accept in a country (France) where the tightest networks depend on which school one went to. Sometimes even a whole career was not enough to overcome the initial handicap, and those not part of these networks obviously harboured a deep level of resentment. This was the reverse of the position in the English-speaking world, where networks are all formed through a person's working life, where they are encouraged and approved of.

Here are a few illustrations:

> *'Here, all of the flexibility comes from your relationships. It's OK for me, because I was at the right school, and since I've been here five or six years, I can find my way around this jumbled organization.'*

> *'No doubt about it: if you want to get on, here, you've got to be part of the right network. That's how it is. If you're on the outside, you don't have a chance.'*

> *'In this department, it's a sum of political and interpersonal games. One would need to transfer people every three years, for example, to break up the fiefdoms, break up all those old-boy networks and bring in some fresh blood. And there's zero mobility. Everything takes place by co-optation and networking.'*

Hardly surprisingly, this organization's labour productivity was low, given the time it took to find relevant information, since compiling it depended on the goodwill of the people involved. Admittedly, everyone admitted that the work got done, a little like the French railwaymen who marvelled 'and yet the trains run!' in their erratic organization. However, the conditions, in terms of time and quality, were dreadful. This was a sore point for the department, and those it dealt with did not hesitate to point this out.

To sum up, we noted at the beginning of this analysis that the actors in this organization were contented on the whole. This contentment stemmed primarily from the protection afforded by the segmented, sequential nature of the work that was a feature of this department. However, it came at a price of all those distortions described above, which represented its cost. The choice – and it was a choice – was to emphasize the organization's internal logic (endogeneity) at the expense of the mission (exogeneity) in a manner somewhat reminiscent of a government department. Once again, work had been allowed to slip out of control.

Silos, or the experts' paradise

On closer inspection, we find that 'letting work slip out of control' through the emergence of a protective silo-type organization was not necessarily an act of resignation in the face of employee pressure, as in the previous chapter. It can also be a response to a situation in which the 'technical' location of the organization is so important that it overshadows all the rest. For anyone familiar with the world of management consultants, for example, this is a frequent occurrence, but this is also the case for any company where the experts (sometimes called 'the professionals', as if everyone else were an 'amateur') take control of management in the name of pre-eminence of their expertise. In other words, the expert executive becomes the managing executive. Yet everyone knows that being good in one's area of excellence is no guarantee of special competence in the field of management.

However, this is what happened in this department, given that the specialized insurance business is increasingly technical. Progress in mathematics, backed up by ever more powerful computer systems, enabled insurers to design more and more complex products (similar to what the now celebrated 'traders' did). At the same time, their mathematical models were becoming increasingly complex. That was the main focus of senior management's attention and effort, especially since the company was in a period of expansion that left little time for anything else, certainly not for the day-to-day running of the organization or thinking about how to adapt it to its mission.

What is more, the primacy afforded to the technical aspects of the business over the smooth running of the organization was accentuated by the general logic of the company, which was naturally focused on short-term performance. 'Reporting' had become the key activity; this was what senior management demanded and what gave the department its visibility. As a result, the department's managers were constantly looking 'upwards' to the people demanding the reports rather than downwards to the organization itself.

Understandably, the technical nature of the business and upwards aspiration combined to turn questions about how the organization works not into minor questions, but simply into questions no one perceived, or at best into questions that never made it onto the agenda. This brings us back to this organization's 'systemic' mode of operation: the department was run by a technically highly qualified management, respected by those that dealt with it, yet it was far more 'upward-looking' towards its superiors than interested in the everyday aspects of the organization. The latter issue was consequently non-existent, as a result of which its actors at best ignored each other and turned in on themselves, or at worst bent the rules of the system to protect themselves, gaining their autonomy and avoiding the constraints inherent in any form of cooperation. The situation lent legitimacy not only to all of its critics, but also to all forms of outside manipulation, especially from those whom the department's mission disturbed the most. This is a recurring situation in similar organizations, those whose low level of integration allows their partners – or clients – to become their true integrating factor and, needless to say, to make them 'pay the price' for playing this integrating role.[3]

In the final analysis, in the case of this department, we ended up with a kind of 'negative federation', in which the actors acknowledged their management's technical competence and its human qualities, but at the same time flatly denied its managerial capabilities. Everyone put this situation down to a problem of 'communication'. In fact, it was a dual problem of management and its mode of functioning.

*

We come now to a second case of managerial dereliction (or managerial sloth), leading once again to the dominance of a 'silo'-based mode of operation, with all that entails, as we are now beginning to perceive. In addition, this case is especially interesting as it serves to illustrate a comment made in the Introduction, namely that life inside companies should not be seen in purely black and white terms. It is a world of contrasts, and we are now about to see how the protective function afforded by these silos can quickly reach its limits when it ends up creating an intolerable gulf between the results it produces (quality in particular) and the demands of the environment.

For this case study, we are now going to visit Northern Europe to observe life in a company that long enjoyed a monopoly situation in its home country in the treatment and distribution of water. For some years, as markets opened up, the company lost its monopoly and became part of a major international corporation that is a world leader in this line of business.[4]

By listening to this company's management team and understanding their daily working situation, it was possible to gain an insight into their confusion and their occasional bitterness. They were unqualified in their radical critique of all aspects of life in the company: its strategy, its organization, its management, its limitations and its membership of a major corporation ('Group'). Rather classically, this attack on the 'fundamentals' masked what ought to be the essential factor, namely the company's performance, its results and its capacity to diversify its businesses. Yet this was not the case at all! Spontaneously, these senior executives insisted on all that was negative, on 'what wasn't working', without producing any cogent solutions liable to improve the situation they viewed as confused and out of control. Each of them had an idea, his own idea, but no more than that.

This apparent contradiction between positive economic results and a negative perception of everyday life should be seen as a signal: it draws attention to the simple fact that these actors – who, it should be repeated, were senior executives – no longer understood 'what was going on'. The environment in which the company operated was progressively moving away from its own environment, and above all from the one it had known in the past. In a word, nostalgia for the 'good old days' was obscuring excellent results, especially so since these had been achieved in working conditions perceived as an endless deterioration of the executives' own conditions: the elites had grown weary. Not surprisingly, here again we encountered the problem of a breakdown in the traditional exchange that linked the executives to their company. Two of the interviewees graphically described this shift from one world to another, from the stability of a dominant position to a situation of precariousness – doubtless more psychological than real – even if it was true that the balance of power had shifted significantly in favour of the Group, i.e., the actors outside the company:

'With us, the water business has always been stable, very stable even. It isn't anymore, and that's worrying people. Before, all one had to do was treat the water and distribute it. Now everything is becoming more complicated. The context has changed. The Group sets policy, and these are no longer the policies we would have set on the spot.'

'I started with a small water board. It was local ... a small group ... close at hand ... quick, decisions were taken rapidly. In recent years, it's become a company dominated by financial concerns, less technical, even at ground level. The rationale behind the decisions now is financial,

because a banker works with money. Forget about the links with the personnel who actually do the work. And the Group has accentuated this financial logic still further.'

So this 'new deal' had difficulty gaining acceptance, especially since no accompanying effort was made to adapt the organization as a result: the 'matrix' structure remained, as its name suggests, as a structure and nothing changed in terms of its everyday mode of operation in silos. This formed the daily reality. Probably a more transversal, cross-perspective approach and cooperation would have been a more appropriate response to the market's new demands, increasingly focused on the search for 'solutions' and no longer simply on a product, even if that product was water. Consequently, the management team became lost in the thickets of an organization ill-adapted to a strategy, which in any case it had difficulty understanding. Senior management took a dim view of this, made its opinion known and blamed the 'malaise' on individuals rather than on the 'system' within which they functioned. Thus, it is worth taking a closer look at this sense of abandonment prevalent among the members of the management team and at their strategies for protecting themselves against this stressful situation.

Birth of a sense of abandonment

Observation of everyday life in this organization in fact revealed a double sense of abandonment, both strategic and organizational: strategic, since there was a dominant impression that the future of the 'core business' had been left to their fate, which was indeterminate for the time being; and organizational, since each individual shared the feeling that the company's day-to-day processes were inexorably breaking down. The mechanism at work here was an interesting one, one I have found in practically all of the companies that have had to cope more and less brutally with the transitions prompted by deregulation and the search for a new 'strategic positioning'.

In the present instance, the managers were having to deal with deregulation and its consequences at the same time as being sucked into the more global strategy of the Group they had become part of – indeed, of which they had become prominent executives. Their starting postulate was that the members of the 'management team', being senior executives, ought by definition to understand these developments and their consequences, and hence be able to embrace them. What had happened was the reverse, predictably refuting this 'theoretical' postulate: these executives embraced nothing at all and merely adopted an attitude of 'anxious criticism'.

As a result, this team – which, as the reader will have grasped, was a team in name only – made no effort to exert control over its own future. In a traditional context, where everything was highly predictable, it had been accustomed to not having to deal with this question. As such, the team looked to its 'chiefs', those who ought to have been the guarantors of this formerly protective world, and found they were already somewhere else. Seen in this way, the demand for a clear strategy for the company should be seen as a plea in favour of reducing this uncertainty, which was starting to put its future in jeopardy, and for greater predictability as to the future of the individuals concerned. This also explains why becoming part of an international group was seen more as a problem than as an opportunity. As always, we see the emergence of the traditional suspicions as to the Group's motives, seen as having an exclusively financial strategy absorbing the attention and energy of all of the top managers and hence that of the company, given the responsibilities these top managers had been given at Group level. This focalization on financial aspects came at the expense of the technical dimension, namely treatment and production, hitherto practically the overriding concern of the company. On top of this came more trivial considerations that served to exacerbate the existing frustration, e.g., the need to cut costs and align wages with market rates, which was not to the advantage of the company's executives. The top executives, now living and operating in a different sphere, handled all of this with nothing but growing irritation. In other words, whether justified or otherwise, this sense of abandonment as to the company's future in the world, and of being part of a Group they had difficulty understanding, nurtured the sense of malaise permeating the 'management team'. This was amplified by the fact that the organization was increasingly ill-adapted, a fact that everyone, senior executives and managers alike, condemned, while at the same time placing the blame on others.

This organization was meant to lead to a 'matrix' organization (another favourite term in the managerial vocabulary). But this was never really implemented, with the result that the 'silos' and their daily consequences for the functioning of the company persisted. This came as anything but a surprise: insofar as none of the players took it upon himself to adapt the organization to its strategy (theoretically the minimum requirement of managerial action), the local actors naturally opted for endogenous protection rather than the harshness of the exogenous world. This, we now know, is a 'classic' reaction. The case before us is an interesting one because it is hard for the outside observer to grasp whether effort really was made to institute a 'matrix' mode of working, such was the confusion surrounding the question. This confusion was not a sign of individuals who had not understood the new 'rules of the game' and therefore unwittingly sabotaged the affair; rather, it testified to the growing disconnect within the company between its formal structure and the way it actually worked. The 'matrix' existed on paper, but its implementation clashed with the 'autonomist' tendencies of the silos (another classic situation), as well as with the frequent tendency of the top executives to short-circuit processes in their search for quick answers and 'responsiveness'. A senior executive summed up the situation as follows:

> '*At a certain point in time(!), our company adopted the matrix. But people never really entered into the spirit of things, out of concern for their local independence. The cross-divisional functions never really played their role, and local management profited from the situation to preserve its autonomy. It wasn't a question of communication, simply that no one, from the top down, ever set an example.*'

The persistence of silos produced the customary results: the decision-making process was long and chaotic, and application of decisions was uncertain. The actors' response to this uncertainty – which undermined their position and could even render them accountable for the outcome of this 'unmanaged' form of work – was to take cover in every possible way: they consulted everyone until they thought they reached a fragile consensus. Needless to say, this further encumbered the decision-making process, but it reassured managers constantly wondering whether they had indeed consulted with and informed everyone, and whether they themselves had read all of the emails in their inbox. Just listen to what one of them had to say:

> *'We spend a lot of time making sure our decisions are secure. Our practices are highly cumbersome, since one has to have consulted everyone. That makes it extremely stressful when you put that in the context of all of the demands coming from the Group. Email has expanded enormously as result, with absolutely no discipline. I can assure you it's a system that's mentally exhausting for everybody.'*

This first-hand account calls for comment. So far, we have emphasized that this silo-based method of working is both protective for individuals and detrimental to organizations in terms of cost and quality. This is verified once again in this instance. But we find too that this protective function reaches its limits when the organization becomes part of a larger body that puts it under permanent pressure. One can see why: to produce its protective effects to the full, segmentation needs to occur in an environment where the company is dominant, thus leaving the environment no choice. Once this balance of power is overturned (e.g., as a result of market opening) or once the body of which it is now just a part has the means to demand more, the phenomenon of suffering in the workplace re-emerges. This no doubt explains why this 'silo' theme is so central, by a long chalk, in our interviews with actors who had hitherto been its beneficiaries. The fact is that they had become counterproductive at every level, as it were: they were weakening the company in its dealings with outside customers (the consumers of water) because we know they are incompatible with a genuine 'client circuit' and thus mechanically jeopardize the quality of service as perceived by customers. These actors are all the more discontented inasmuch as they are driven to express their dissatisfaction through 'politicians', only too happy to wreak their revenge on a company that until then had made customers pay the price of its monopoly position. In a sense, the company had put itself in a position of weakness in an environment already unfavourable to it. In turn, this disturbing outside critique, to which the managers were neither accustomed nor prepared, was shattering the already fragile work community, further depressing a gloomy climate and irritating a top management team unable to obtain from its managers what it thought it had a right to expect.

The work community implodes

As we have seen, this implosion of the work community, brought about by a mode of operation no longer adapted to the altered demands of an open market, primarily concerns the 'customer relationship'. This sensitive subject, symbolizing how unsuited this organization is to a deregulated market,[5] also carried significant threats for the future, further fuelling anxieties that were already acute and bolstering the idea that the strategy was unclear, indeed non-existent, in the eyes of some. This is how one manager expressed this 'systemic feedback loop':

> *'We're clear in principle, on certain points, on our vision vis-à-vis the client for example. But when you try to transpose this to the organization, it suddenly becomes less clear. No one is responsible from start to finish. At the level of 'customer service' one is directed towards processes, i.e., internally. That's a great nuisance. And on the management side, there's a split between sales and customer service, with two managers, each minding his bailiwick. There's no one there to encourage cooperation.'*

One could hardly put it better!

Therefore, the 'silos' became a major cause of confusion and mutual incomprehension. It wasn't that the senior managers hadn't understood that the world had changed: they could not fail to observe that market opening was a fact, and it was hard to see how this could be rolled back in the foreseeable future. The problem lay in the way in which this organization had been abandoned, how it had fallen apart and, ultimately, how its sense of community had given way to new strategies of protection. The uncompromising response of top management – its criticisms levelled at its own lower level managers – had served more as an accelerator than as a moderator, by giving the latter the feeling that their senior managers had broken ranks with their 'home town'. Their response to this was a highly typical withdrawal, a traditional response to the breakdown of the 'implicit deal' that customarily binds a company to its managers. In the old world, the latter 'counted' quite simply because they were managers. For them it spelled a good salary and social status. In the new world, they had difficulty coming to terms with the fact that they were now just numbers, a word that has given very concrete meaning to the madness of processes. As one of them said, appalled:

> *'We have an identification number now! When I started at head office I must have given it I don't know how many times. It's a slightly odd way to identify people, all the same!'*

Likewise, this strategy has led to a 'honeycomb' mode of working, as described in the previous case: each person works on his own, paying little attention to others, with information flowing neither up nor down. As a result, each person 'interprets' decisions according to his own interests and applies them – or not – while the content and legitimacy of these decisions diminishes as they circulate around the organization.

Alongside withdrawal, though, another strategy was emerging, this time being implemented by the most dynamic of the senior managers. Here, in what I call the 'market strategy', the 'dynamic' individuals, who were also the youngest managers, were quick to grasp that they could expect little from the organization in terms of helping them obtain what they needed in order to perform the missions entrusted to them. Their response was to 'help themselves', 'shopping' around for available human resources. They attract around them the people they consider to be the most competent and sideline the others. They reconstitute their own firm within the firm, their logic being what they themselves describe as an 'Anglo-American'-style meritocracy. They see no limit to this exercise, since the honeycomb mode described above implies a climate of 'every man for himself' for anyone wanting to move things (his things) forward. As one of them puts it:

> *'We are moving towards a mode of working that's slowly improving. We're trying to modernize the way we work, and things are getting better. For my own projects, I recruit internally and externally as it suits me. And my bosses too give me these jobs informally. It isn't a problem. One soon gets used to it.'*

This is an interesting paradox in this company, which initially opted to 'protect' its employees in general, and its managers in particular, by granting them the full autonomy that comes with a silo-based organization. But this then broke up of its own accord under pressure from a market that was undergoing far-reaching change. At the end of this process, which plunged the older managers into confusion and anxiety, a new mode of working emerged emphasizing personal initiative, with the 'smartest operators' grabbing territory left vacant by the senior managers. The latter, meanwhile, had been 'sucked upwards' to the Group level, to build a kind of federation of executives virtually operating like the self-employed, beyond any real control. This is delightful from the point of view of the actors' intelligence, but it also shows just how hard it can be to get a grip on work again once it has slipped out of control.

3
We've Let the Customer Get Away

What's this? The customer, who is supposed to be the focus of all our attention, real or supposed; he is the overall victor in the process of globalization and the resulting market opening; the person who, thanks to the Internet, is supposed to enjoy limitless choice. Yet here we are claiming he has been left to his own devices? This is hard to believe, given the avalanche of advertising telling us how much companies love and cherish the customer, and how accustomed we are to all that managerial vocabulary that speaks of nothing but, both through and for the customer. There is even a training course at one of Europe's finest business schools that calls itself 'Building customer-obsessed organizations'. To our grandparents, the customer was king. For us, he has become an obsession. It's almost funny.

However, this somewhat overblown rhetoric obscures developments that are perfectly consistent with the theme of this book. To recapitulate: work has been allowed to 'get away' in an economic context where the client had little choice and where, to put it another way, it was the product that was scarce. Whoever 'controlled' the product, i.e., whoever produced or distributed it, wielded unchecked power to impose his own logic and constraints on the client; the latter, meanwhile, only too happy to acquire this scarce product, had no option but to thank the vendor. This was the golden age of bureaucracies, with nothing to oblige them to take account of the customer's needs when designing their work processes.

The priority enjoyed by the producer at the client's expense explains how the work process drifted out of control, via the mechanisms of externalization, as described in the previous chapters. I won't go back over this. However, one can see how this unequal producer/buyer relationship, which many thought was here to stay and was unlikely to be challenged, was in fact fragile and short-lived. Were the relationship to be reversed (as happened), the client would surely perceive it and seek advantages that had previously been beyond reach. He would start by 'roaming' from supplier to supplier in search of his own consumer Garden of Eden. The mobile telephone sector is a prominent example of this transformation: people coming from the provinces to live in Paris in the 1960s had to wait two years, on average, for a fixed telephone line. This was considered a privilege at the time, distributed by a ministry enjoying a monopoly situation. Nowadays we all know how impatient a teenager will be if his cellphone isn't activated instantaneously at the moment of purchase.

We sometimes have difficulty grasping just what a revolution this was for companies, a process that has percolated through to certain government departments. Like it or not, this 'reversal of scarcity' between product and client put the latter back at the heart of the debate, and much more forcefully so than some simplistic accounts would have us believe. This is because, during those halcyon days when the client counted for little, ultimately, he was left to his own devices. In particular, companies were more concerned at the time with showering benefits on their workers than on giving priority to an actor bereft of real power. To put it another way, while letting work slip away, companies were also letting the customer slip away! They were unable or unwilling to deal simultaneously with their employees and their customers.

Abandoning the client

As a result, customer management was 'subcontracted' out, as if it were a minor activity that could be entrusted to peripheral players. Here again, let's not be naïve: this remains the dominant model to this day, not a marginal case. Who, today, can send out one of his acknowledged top players to go and face the customer? So difficult is this for companies, even though they see the need, that they have begun to 'get smart' with their customers. They send out letters signed by a senior executive, with a phone number that ends up at some delocalized call centre.

The customer is subcontracted out – abandoned, in a sense – in a variety of ways. The first and most obvious is to outsource the sales function to outside bodies such as distributors of various stripes. That is what the makers of home appliances did in France, progressively abandoning their scanty distribution networks in favour of the big chain stores. This proved to be catastrophic for them. The big chain stores, citing French legislation prohibiting a refusal to sell (this has since been amended), 'grabbed' the brands and used these brands for their own ends, employing familiar sales techniques. The resulting monopoly they established over the customer relationship allowed the chain stores to assert their power over the manufacturers, gradually driving them out of the market in favour of higher margin outside brands. The customer wasn't better served, but he did become more profitable for the distributors ...

Yet, other strategies were available and Japanese producers took the opposite tack to that taken by the French. Rather than let some large, threatening distributor get hold of the consumer, they themselves financed the distributors, leaving them in a state of weakness that robbed them of any autonomy vis-à-vis the national manufacturers and preventing them from even trying to grab the customer. Admittedly, the Japanese were helped by their government regulations (with their Fair Trade Committee), which consistently favoured national producers to the detriment of foreign operators seeking to enter the market. This drove up the cost of market entry and forced anyone prepared to take the risk of setting foot there to enter into agreement with a national producer, who naturally made sure to confine the newcomer to a niche market. In the case of France, the newcomer was best advised to forge an alliance with a powerful distributor that controlled the customer by offering the distributor the attractive margins mentioned above. Clearly, the long-term stakes are high when it comes to controlling the customer.

It was in order to avoid these pitfalls that companies sought, and found, a different way to outsource the client. This time, they outsourced clients to parts of their own organizations (such as sales representatives and counsellors), placing them in the position of 'influential outsiders', both *inside* and *outside* the organization. The positions of these people grow stronger as the market situation goes into reverse. Beyond the often-exaggerated legitimacy accorded to the 'person on the ground', i.e., in direct contact with the client or user, this situation gives these people real power inside the organization. They will therefore do everything they can to hold on to it, spinning a halo around their activities and weaving personal, rather than organizational, ties with clients. For example, that is what happens with postal workers who deliver items of great value to those who take delivery of them (mail and newspapers). In one sense, they have successfully reversed the notion of 'client': in any other activity, 'client' refers to the person who pays for the good or service sold to him, hence the stock phrase 'I'm the one who's paying'. For the postal worker, the client is not the person who pays: the 'client' is the recipient, and in this case the recipient 'receives' the service (i.e., letters and packages) free of charge! The resulting relationship is particularly friendly and satisfying insofar as no money changes hands, the financial transaction having taken place 'elsewhere', at the time of dispatch. The postal worker is then free to organize his time as he likes, and then manages the relationship with his client – to whom this service costs nothing – as he sees fit.

Needless to say, these situations make the company vulnerable by depriving it of complete control over what the market is offering, since the person to whom it has – incautiously – delegated control over this is more interested in selling what he knows than in giving the customer what he needs or what the company has to offer. That is why good *personal* relationships between this client and the account manager are no guarantee of success, contrary to what salespeople would have us believe these days.

As often happens, people think that technology will bring salvation, which amounts to seeking a technical solution to a human problem. This is a constant temptation for companies, but it is a high-risk strategy with no guarantee of success. Companies nevertheless set about computerizing their sales staff's work with a plethora of hardware and sophisticated software; little by little this took control of this population, which now looks into the office just to 'gossip with the secretaries'. I won't repeat here the sorry tale of difficulties and occasional failures encountered by these strategies, particularly in the pharmaceutical industry. These difficulties illustrate the extent to which control over the client is a key challenge for organizations, after having previously treated them as marginal. The captive client, thus subcontracted, has become a major source of uncertainty in a competitive market, and winning him back will be tough proposition. Here again, managerial sloth comes at a high price.

The first case study in the following section illustrates the point. Again we travel to Northern Europe, and for the first time we enter the world of government.[1] In managing the representation of its economic interests abroad, the country in question was faced with a common problem when managing change in the public sector – namely, how to persuade personnel to change the way they work, undergo serious evaluation and agree to share the information that constitutes their personal 'added value' within their organization. The issue was further complicated by the fact that this concerned 'commercial counsellors' in the said government's embassies and consulates. This amounted to a sizeable population of 1,200, only 200 of whom were diplomats (and thus civil servants), the remainder being 'locally engaged' staff working in their home country for the country in question. Finally, this department (as we will call it from now on) was confronted with two difficulties: first, it did not directly manage any of its members, either those at head office or those in the field, since this was administered by the other ministerial unit that had been connected with it since its inception, making it a kind of 'virtual organization'; and, second, the department had no tradition of 'systematic reporting', since the diplomatic corps had no results-based culture, and indeed interviewees never regarded this issue as a priority.

Caution with ambiguity

The department foresaw serious drawbacks, and even distinct opposition, when introducing the Customer Relationship Management (CRM) system it was now contemplating under pressure from the Finance Ministry in order to avoid seeing its funding reduced or even stopped altogether. This CRM system was intended to compile information on the counsellors' activities: whom did they contact? How often? For what purpose? What did they talk about and what were the tangible results of their conversations? And, more generally, what were the key things to bear in mind about the people they met?

On a second level, it is obvious that this kind of system could be a good way to obtain greater insight into what these people do and, to be frank, to ascertain the true amount of work performed, a matter on which the department had some misgivings. The resulting information could then pave the way for a general restructuring, modifying the allocation of human resources and transferring the bulk of these from the 'old countries' (i.e., European countries), where the stakes are low, towards the emerging countries, the BRICs[2] especially, where efforts and investment now need to be focused.

Consequently, we can see why this is not just a question of introducing a new technology, since that is neutral, with no direct impact on the organization, i.e., on the way people work. We have long known that all 'technical systems' have a far-reaching impact on the way organizations function, and that they can change the power relationships between the different actors. In the case before us here, not only was the introduction of transparency into what people did genuinely problematic, but these people saw the attempt to shine a light on what they did as a real threat, regardless of the country they worked in, and this last point should be stressed.[3]

A handful of observations will convey some idea of what really goes on in these representations. To begin with, at the time of the survey, the degree of knowledge about the CRM system was highly variable and in some cases very weak. Except for those in embassies where the system had been tested, counsellors had 'heard about it' but had received no serious information. This was partly because each counsellor worked in isolation from the others and there were few occasions at which views could be shared. Their superiors never got together for a general meeting, and nor, *a fortiori*, did the counsellors; in addition, the 'locally engaged' counsellors never had an opportunity to visit the head office. As a result, their attitude was a cautious one of 'wait and see'.

Perhaps even more importantly, it quickly became clear that, contrary to the fears expressed by the project's instigators, the local actors did not imagine that the department could use the system 'against them'. In fact, when they did express a view about those who would be using the new system or those for whom this system might be useful, they spoke about themselves, not about the department. In their minds, they would be the main users, the ones who would benefit from this innovation. They therefore perceived it in *technical* terms and were only concerned as to whether it would be useful to them in their day-to-day work. For example, they saw no way in which the head office might use the CRM system to introduce greater centralization.

This might be considered a highly positive situation, with local units trusting their organization and harbouring no suspicions as to the ulterior motives of their superiors or suspecting any dissembled strategy. Surely, though, the reality was slightly different. As the analysis proceeded, it became clear that the counsellors were even less open than expected to any kind of evaluation, whether by this system or by any other means. The idea of evaluation itself was simply foreign to their mental universe, to say nothing of the possibility that it might serve as a basis for introducing a new system of pay. As, mentioned earlier, there was no results-based culture in this environment. Worse still, if one can put it that way: the idea of linking evaluation to pay was simply bad mannered! From this it flowed that the gap between 'head office' and the local units was probably wider than anyone had previously imagined. This was clearly a dangerous situation, since it highlighted the total lack of transparency as to the real objectives of this initiative, other than for a handful of high-ranking diplomats, to whom this was of little concern. Right from the outset of my investigation, I had to emphasize that in prolonging this ambiguous situation, there was a risk of triggering an extremely fierce response on the part of actors if they suddenly gained the impression – justifiably, as it happened – that they had been led up the garden path. This came as all the more of a surprise and a shock to them inasmuch as the existing systems of evaluation – to the extent that these existed at all – were bureaucratic in nature. There was a 'process' for setting objectives (which was in any case rather vague), with a twice-yearly review, although this had no repercussions on the fate of or compensation for the individuals concerned. In any case, the 'variable portion' of their pay was universally regarded as insignificant.

One last observation: none of the interviewees with managerial responsibilities mentioned the evaluation of his subordinates as forming part of his remit.

The above remarks allow us to understand the counsellors' concerns with regard to the new system. What they hoped for in the first place was that it would be easy to use (insofar as the technical aspect of the system was concerned), in terms of the time needed to connect, enter the data and find worthwhile information. They already had some idea of how this would work, again from a test country, which left them with the impression that there was quite a lot of room for improvement in order to ensure an acceptable level of ease of use.

The second question they raised was a curious one, touching on a more sensitive subject: how could it be possible to enter every aspect of their activity into a system like this? There was general agreement in describing this as being 'intangible' on occasion. Their work consisted of attending social events, including dinners, gala evenings, cultural events and impromptu meetings with people who were part of their 'network' – more precisely, it emerged that the higher the rank of the counsellors (particularly the 'locals'), the more they considered that the most important part of their work was intangible and therefore difficult to measure. Indeed, the same people pointed out that not only was it unwise to try to measure of their activity, but that attempting to measure their results would be even more unreliable. They cited many examples – most of them highly sophisticated – of the types of event that they attended, the information they derived from them, obtained from their personal relationships, making it impossible to measure the results obtained. They further pointed out that some of their interlocutors, particularly companies approaching or contacting the department, had learnt how to 'manipulate' it in order to obtain more and more from it, naturally without mentioning what they had already obtained from a particular counsellor. Only the lowest-ranking counsellors took a positive view of the use of this system, but since they never 'got out', and never met people, there was nothing at stake for them.

This is the background that allowed us to understand these counsellors' strategies in the face of a threat which, though rarely stated explicitly, was clearly at the back of the minds of the people concerned. Beyond the differences in their careers and reasons for joining the service, there was a tacit agreement among them that no one should get in anyone else's way. For high-ranking diplomats such as the Consuls-General, for example, being in charge of this 'commercial' activity was a short-term stint under Foreign Ministry rules, which gave them responsibility for overseeing these counsellors. For the 'locals', working for this department enabled them to find work on the spot. They derived considerable power from their local roots, their networks and their unique capacity to clear up problems that could not be resolved through the official channels. Indeed, this was why they were recruited, why the authorities wanted them to stay and why nobody bothered them.

All this goes to confirm the observer's view that the pace of work was not all that demanding, especially since no one 'tried too hard', with the potential risk of a 'shake-up'. In other words, we are dealing with a perfectly classical government department where the actors agreed that each of them must enjoy a high degree of freedom, avoiding all outside interference. It was a somewhat featureless environment, where people spoke little, with no real team spirit, other than to maintain a high level of protection vis-à-vis the outside. So there was nothing special about this picture: as in any bureaucracy, routine relations between individuals were distant, but they were capable of closing ranks effectively the moment they spotted an outside threat to the existing equilibrium. Digging deeper, however, three strategies emerged, which not surprisingly corresponded to three different positions within the organization.

Three examples of protection strategies

The first of these strategies concerned counsellors working in their country of residence. Consequently, they were not 'expats' in the normal sense of the term, insofar as they were working in this country as a matter of choice, and they felt some bitterness about this. They had considerable misgivings as to the advantages of the CRM system, even though they did not know much about it. With a large dose of cynicism, they pointed out that this was not the first time that people had tried to introduce a handful of changes into the way these positions were administered, with catastrophic results each time. They cited numerous examples to justify their preference for the previous system, where everything was 'done by hand' and which each counsellor configured the system to suit his own needs; this was no doubt simpler, but also surely more effective than any centralized system, in their view at least. And even if these 'local systems' were incapable of communicating with each other, all agreed that the existing system was largely sufficient for their needs. What is more, they considered their central administration to be incapable of managing something on this scale, which was at the same time inefficient and highly complex to use. In other words, they cited previous failures as excellent grounds for opposing the present attempts for change. In so doing, they were protecting their autonomy and their territory. Moreover, it was they who placed the greatest emphasis on the notion of 'intangible activities' and explained why they could not be 'fed into' a computer and, still less, measured. For the same reasons, it was they who provided the most details and examples in explaining why the results of their activities were not measurable, especially not mechanically and bureaucratically. In other words, what they knew, what they did and the people they met concerned them, and them alone. Sharing this knowledge would amount to a loss of power, with the possible risk that at some point someone might cast doubt on their utility to the organization. As a result, these actors were practically impossible to 'convince', not because they did not 'understand' (psychologically speaking) but because they had no interest in the deployment of the new system (sociologically speaking). They therefore employed a variety of resistance strategies, setting conditions, putting up objections and continuously citing additional technical problems.

The second group, the higher rank 'locally engaged' staff, chiefly in the emerging countries, wielded considerable power since they controlled relations with the local bureaucrats, businesspeople and, more generally, with everyone who counted within their territory. Their assets were highly personal, generally resulting from their family's long-established presence in the local community. They had often built on this personal heritage with excellent qualifications from one or more universities in the West. Although 'Westernized', they were still integrated into local society, being familiar with its customs, unwritten rules and social codes. They enjoyed direct access to the most useful networks in order to obtain what was sometimes unobtainable, or painfully slow to obtain, via the normal channels. Finally, they were perfectly aware that all of this constituted the essence of their value to their employer.

However, this value was not rewarded in the existing organization. Under the bureaucratic rules governing the way personnel was administered, they could only keep their job if they were prepared to countenance very small, if not to say insignificant, pay rises. And these tiny increases, sometimes in the form of symbolic bonuses, in no way compensated for the absence of any prospect of promotion, since they were not citizens of the country in which they worked. Stuck where they were, they intended to stay there come what may, and regardless of what they contributed to the organization. Because the department did not oversee its own personnel, its impact on their career prospects was very small. These people, then, had gone as high as they could.

This situation might seem highly paradoxical and damaging, but in fact, in the process of framing a change strategy, some room for manoeuvre began to emerge. This was because these actors, particularly the younger ones among them, clearly evinced their willingness to do more, sometimes much more, to involve themselves in the daily life of their unit, provided this commitment was rewarded by a win-win contract. This was less a matter of money than of 'opening up opportunities', enabling them to move up the organization's social ladder. Indeed, that is what they meant when talked about the 'stupid personnel administration system' then prevalent in the embassies. The 'uncertainty' they controlled through their mastery of the relevant environment gave them considerable bargaining power with their organization, and they had no intention of relinquishing this merely for the deployment of a new IT system. Events showed that they made use of this – for the greater benefit of the department as a whole.

In doing so, they carried along with them all or some of the others, especially the lower ranking local hires. These locally hired people did not even control the organization's 'clients', for most of them spent their time in the office doing routine translation or document production work. Consequently, they had developed a 'follower' strategy, devoid of any particular commitment, more interested in their personal lives than in the effective running of their unit. In the course of the interviews, they clearly showed that they desired no particular recognition and were not contemplating promotion. Their job with this unit was a way to live in the city and stay within their milieu, not to satisfy any financial ambitions. Their perception of the CRM system was positive, *a priori*, as it could help them in their daily work when this sometimes entailed receiving information from units elsewhere; it could also raise the profile of their contribution on occasion, which was hitherto largely ignored by the other actors. Ultimately, they had nothing particular at stake regarding the use of the system, since they controlled nothing unique and were thus indispensable to the life of this community.

Therefore, the organization was obliged to bargain with those who mastered and monopolized access to the client in order to reassert control over the conduct of its own activities. In fact, power had shifted so far down to the local level that it could not negotiate from a position of strength, for it is a fundamental fact of life in organizations that power is not hierarchy. Yet organizations continue to 'look upwards' and often nonchalantly subcontract operational tasks deemed to be of little importance compared with the majesty of framing a strategy.

However, framing strategy, when one has allowed others to gain control over what is essential for the life of the organization, its 'core business', amounts to placing oneself in a highly vulnerable situation and having to pay a high price just to be able to do one's job. Even then, it is necessary to have something in hand in order to bargain with those who wield the real power, which may be impossible if all the latter want is to preserve their autonomy.

Winning back power through integration

Winning back power over actors or units, once their control of the client has made them autonomous, is part of what firms call 'moving towards greater integration'. It is worth taking a closer look at this trend, given that until now the rhetoric of decentralization has tended to dominate. Decentralization was supposed to instil 'entrepreneurial' behaviour in ever-expanding units, with local individual initiative expected to compensate for the trend towards bureaucracy in the new behemoths born as a result of mergers and acquisitions in particular. One could draw an amusing parallel between this determination to maintain units with considerable capacity to take initiatives and all the contemporary talk about 'autonomous work groups' when referring to workers on the factory floor. In both cases, local initiative won out over 'global alignment'. What makes the two approaches identical is that both are contextual. They have grown up in economic environments where companies had sufficient resources to cover the costs generated by the individuals' or units' autonomy. It is worth recalling that the reason why we now call less for autonomy than for cooperation is because the latter is seen as a vehicle for cost-cutting.

With resources becoming progressively scarcer, strenuous efforts have been made to 'pool' things such as services to control and harmonize processes that companies euphemistically refer to as 'integration'. Make no mistake, this is the overriding concern on both sides of the Atlantic in the early twenty-first century (the emerging countries have benefited from the learning curves of developed countries), regardless of the sector of activity. Bankers are just as eager to integrate as aircraft engine and submarine turbine manufacturers, and service-providing firms are no less enthusiastic.

The curious observer may (justifiably) raise the occasional eyebrow at this fierce determination on the part of companies to make sure everything is done the same way everywhere. The desire to make everything work in the same way so that order prevails over disorder is not motivated by 'aesthetics' or just to satisfy some control freak. Although Robert Reich has shown us that the present-day organization of firms stems from the fact that they were all run by military men at the end of the Second World War,[4] that is not what we are talking about! Integration is a mechanism designed to take back the control ceded during the golden years. One can see why the actors concerned have misgivings over this, especially since it entails regaining control of relations with a client who, as we shall see later, demands ever more integrated solutions, which units focused on a single product are hard put to supply. Being more integrated, then, means losing autonomy and sharing the client that is the most priceless asset guaranteeing that autonomy.

All these difficulties in applying this integration are illustrated by the case of a world leader in complex electrical installations. This 'global' firm[5] set about overhauling its sales approach, shifting from its initial approach, which was highly focused on the products it manufactured and distributed, to a more client-driven logic embracing the solutions clients demanded. There is nothing surprising about this approach: despite the misgivings it aroused within the firm, we saw that it was an intrinsic part of a change process occurring in all sectors of the market economy, with the notable exception of those (still) in a monopoly position. Companies are having to deal with clients who are better and better informed, who have more and more choice, and who have learned to rationalize their purchasing in order to manage their investment as carefully as possible. There was no reason why this company should have been spared these developments.

Indeed, that was what its managers found when they noted that 'small unit business' accounted for three-quarters of revenue (which is to be expected in the electrical equipment sector) and that in this context the only way to identify and grasp opportunities was by staying very close to the client on a day-to-day basis. Similarly, they noted that they had an army of salespeople dealing with a single client, which bred confusion; indeed, it allowed clients to play one sales representative off against the others and to profit from their supplier's low degree of integration. Car manufacturers were the first to grasp the full extent of the dangers in the way they dealt with their suppliers and remedied this by setting up 'technocentres'.

Finally, ever-tougher safety standards for electrical equipment necessitated great care in the use of agents, middlemen, resellers and local fitters. To achieve this, it was necessary to have complete, day-to-day control over the customer relationship and to redefine the means of access to the customer. Management's response was twofold: to delocalize its sales force to move it as close as possible to the client (the force was split between the divisional head offices and the field at the time) and to pool these sales forces in order to cut costs and the number of representatives the client had to deal with.

However, as always in the life of organizations – as in life in general – the intellectual justification for a plan was not enough to make it acceptable to the actors concerned, especially if it entailed pooling sales forces hitherto scattered among the different business units. But this would have undermined the instrument many of the actors concerned used to establish their performance, by which they were evaluated and paid, and on which their promotion prospects depended.

No doubt, this was why interlocutors in the field expressed not the slightest sense of threat to their work, and hence no sense of urgency regarding the project's implementation. But although all were agreed in saying that the firm's organic growth had been flat in recent years, this was never blamed on the fragmented nature of their sales organization. On the contrary, they thought it effective and well-suited to their market. It is easy to see why: it was they who created it and adapted it to the firm's successive reorganizations. Only those actually in charge of the plan seemed to think the clients' needs had evolved. Everyone continued to cling to this vision and the traditional way of doing things. They were just about prepared to admit that the competition had already embarked on a drastic upheaval of its sales organization, but many saw this as merely one of those fads that often take hold in companies.

Consequently, to this day this company still does not have an integrated sales organization. There are people scattered all over the place in an impenetrable maze. This diversity (according to the optimistic view) or unchecked disorder (the pessimistic view) represents an impenetrable barrier to any initiative that needs to be based on a 'shared vision' of the client's needs. As the interviewee below put it:

'What I've heard about the plan is very diffuse and confusing. There's no consensus as to what needs to be done. Some people think we should go ahead, but in reality no one agrees.'

So the debate is both biased and partial. We have seen why it is biased, and it is partial in the sense that the actors involved appear to have grasped only one component of the plan proposed, namely the delocalization of the sales forces. As a result, they overlooked an essential feature of the plan, namely the pooling of the sales forces. Needless to say, this was neither an oversight nor a case of poor communication, but a strategic posture. As the popular saying goes: 'There's none so deaf as those who will not hear.'

That is why the idea of delocalizing the sales forces raised so few problems and was even the subject of an explicit consensus, since it gave recognition to existing practice and above all left the sales autonomy of the 'product lines' intact. Everyone was free to implement it as he saw fit, in the direction of those countries he considered most important to his entity. In other words, it was not predicated on a 'supranational' collective interest any more than it assumed a client wishing to deal with a single interlocutor or to be viewed by the company in the round. Seen thus, this 'delocalization with autonomy' enshrined the primacy given to the product-driven as opposed to the customer-driven approach. It showed that, for the actors in the different units, the idea of moving geographically closer to the client had nothing to do with a new understanding of his needs, and above all nothing to do with the need to take an 'integrated' view of him. It left intact the protective segmentation by 'product lines', which guarded their autonomy through their control over 'their' client all the more jealously: in their eyes, the state of their order book meant there was no need for solidarity or aid from the rest of the company. We are at the antipodes of the dominant managerial rhetoric.

Delocalization is not mutualization

Going further, delocalization clearly acted as a 'strategic alternative' to a possible 'obligation to cooperate' between units, which was, by definition, perceived as a threat. That is why many interviewees said they had 'already implemented the plan' and that any further initiatives would change nothing for them. The most clearsighted among them were just about prepared to mention some technical problems surrounding the delocalization: for example, the fact that the front office was to be delocalized in the different countries, whereas the back office remaining in the country of origin could complicate the task of drafting offers. Similarly, in the units' head offices there were fears of the emergence of a commercial 'sub-proletariat' of people not 'on the ground', who would therefore be obliged to work under the orders of those in daily and direct contact with the client.

Overall, though, and with some slight qualifications relating mainly to the unit's size and 'health', the lack of a sense of urgency or necessity was a powerful obstacle to the plan's acceptance. This strategic posture, which flowed from the fact that the actors were far better at foreseeing the costs (loss of autonomy) than the benefits (expansion of their activity) of the plan, contradicted the feelings of the small minority that had already experienced the pooling of commercial resources. With a few minor qualifications, the latter were highly positive about the change. But the fact remains that, at the time of this study, mistrust and opposition dominated. In particular, the misgivings were not confined to a handful of 'local barons' but were shared among a small group of top managers, even though these managers were supposed to be the guardians of the common good. Even the Executive Committee was in virtual disagreement over everything, in particular over the urgency and necessity of changing the way relations with the client were managed: its members' situations in their respective markets were not identical and they were as parochial in their outlook as their subordinates. This was because, contrary to certain over-hasty visions of life in the company, 'it' did not depend on 'people', but on the ways in which their superiors or their shareholders evaluated them, resulting in turn in these parochial and very short-term responses. Consequently, it was difficult for the plan to establish its legitimacy and stimulate ad hoc alliances.

While few were disturbed by the delocalization, mutualization or pooling was viewed with much scepticism; it aroused caution at best and opposition at worst (and most frequently). The opposition came from the so-called 'classic' units, the heart of the organization. These units failed to see anything in the reform for themselves and wanted to retain total control over their commercial activities. The regional directors (covering a part of the globe), a newly created function to manage this integration process and oversee the different countries, immediately adopted a strategy of seeking to avoid cutting themselves off too quickly from the various units where the power resided for the time being and for an indefinite period to come. Two alliances emerged within the organization, both reflecting hostility to the plan. These alliances illustrated the extent to which the most powerful actors, foreseeing a possible weakening of their position, fought to hold on to what the earlier laxity had allowed them to conquer, and over which they had established a stranglehold.

The first, 'strong', alliance unsurprisingly united countries and units, each seizing the opportunity to escape from the plan's tutelage: the regions in the former case and the business lines (embracing several units) in the latter case. This is a *locus classicus* in the life of a company: the country bosses, who controlled the day-to-day business, fought to defend their territory; the units, meanwhile, attempted to push back against the business lines on which they depended from a vaguely 'corporate' point of view – i.e., in the sense of distinguishing between 'those who spend their time messing things up and those who bring home the bacon'. Moreover, it is worth pointing out that the commercial heads of these divisions were already beating a retreat: I found that they were always both overworked, always away on business trips, yet incapable, during the interviews, of describing in concrete terms what they actually did. This is an unmistakable sign, characteristic of actors who throw themselves into frantic activity to compensate for their lack of effective power over the course of events. We all know how the busiest person in a company is someone with little to do! Here we were dealing with a function that was constantly 'chasing' something: information, contracts and those handling the client relationship. With resistance coming from the countries and the units, the strength of this hostility to the part of the plan that did not suit these actors was palpable.

By comparison, the alliance between the regional directors and the business lines could be seen as 'weak'. Given that the only perceived (and accepted) aspects of the plan were its proposals for delocalization and geographical proximity to the client, this was an alliance of those least affected by it.

Clearly, what determined the positions of all these actors vis-à-vis this 'integrating' plan was a question of turf wars. Actors were 'instrumentalizing' the plan and making highly political use of it, in the etymological sense of word as pertaining to the affairs of the 'city'. The most surprising example was the hostility of some countries to 'top-down' (regional) integration, using the plan to assert their authority over smaller countries that they considered came within their sphere of influence. But what about the business lines eager to take just what they wanted and nothing else, according to their needs, and rejecting mutualization except where they could be the leaders? In a word, the plan could be summed up as consolidating the power of the strongest – a far cry from 'customer focus' and its organizational demands!

Finally, it is worth considering the real possibility of deploying such an integrationist plan in an organization as fragmented as this, especially in the face of actors who argue 'if it ain't broke, don't fix it'. The real argument was not over the plan itself, in which, in the final analysis, no one was truly interested, with the notable exception of a handful of top managers aware of the potential limits to the present way of doing things. The heart of the issue concerned the degree of integration and cooperation people were prepared to accept, which, to be frank, was pretty weak. True 'customer focus', as we have pointed out, is a threat to situations of autonomy that have been conquered over time and taken root in the true source of power, namely effective control over the customer, which has in turn been allowed to evolve into impregnable monopolies. The organization had a choice between waiting for a major crisis to clear the air for a new deal or embarking on protected, tortuous negotiations, leaving the initial project defanged and unrecognizable (it opted for this latter method). Yesterday's complacency makes the cost of change prohibitive today.

Part II
How Companies Lost their Grip (2): Front-line Managers Have Been Sacrificed on the Altar of Intermediate Bureaucracies

4
Sacrificing the Front-line Managers

Front-line managers hold the keys to success: they must be supported, 'recognized' and given the means to run the operations entrusted to them effectively. That this should be a theme companies are now rediscovering is no surprise. It stems from this generalized loss of control that has led today's managements to shun all-devouring bureaucracies in favour of what is now seen as a guarantee of simplicity. 'Toyotism'[1] itself has something to do with this, since it was partly responsible for the birth of the idea that it is the people who are in direct contact with the 'operatives' that can make the best use of them.

Here again, necessity rules. Who better than these intermediate supervisors, who are in closest contact with this much-feared daily reality – namely the client and the task of controlling production and labour costs – to help companies win back the lost ground? Much thought has gone into strategy, a noble discipline if ever there was one; huge resources and brainpower have been invested in financial management, because that is what the markets and financial analysts demanded (and still do). Now we need to turn our attention back to operations, as if we were belatedly rediscovering the virtues of the 'bottom of the pyramid' so dear to the airline SAS Group and its legendary boss, Jan Carlzon. There is a long road ahead! But let's not be naïve: with a little hindsight, this is plainly another swing of the pendulum in the life of organizations.

Initially, they cannot resist the temptation to centralize, but when taken to extremes this produces the reverse of the desired effect: it dilutes effective control over the organization concerned, at which point the need is felt for a return to the grassroots in order to curb the costly (and quality-destroying) effects of the prior phase. That is where the difficulties begin, for this involves challenging vested interests and motivating actors hitherto almost completely ignored.

Can we trust those 'at the bottom of the pyramid'?

The idea of turning to the people 'at the bottom of the pyramid' scarcely comes naturally. Even in the 'new economy', once the pioneer phase is over, companies have been observed to become 'structured' (i.e., hierarchies emerge), as intermediate layers (bureaucracies) proliferate, staff and support functions balloon, and nomenclatures and control processes grow in importance. At that point, power starts to be diluted, as each echelon seeks a piece of it. This gives rise to a paradox that must be addressed once companies start to feel the need to reassert control over what they do. This paradox is that once we get down to the level of the front-line managers, little of this power remains, having drained away in the meanders of the different levels, functions and general rules that leave the local supervisor all too little leeway. Yet at the same time these grassroots workers, operatives or producers of the goods or services the company intends to market still wield considerable power. As we saw earlier, they have the power to set their own pace of work, among other things. How, in that case, are these 'shift foremen', 'shop foremen' and 'plant managers' supposed to go about instilling rigour and discipline in the people they 'supervise', other than through endless, painstaking negotiations from a position of inferiority?

One difficulty is that companies get little help from their human resources (HR) departments. These departments have put up the least resistance to the drive for centralization, having reached an understanding with their main partners, the trade unions, to manage personnel jointly and thereby mutually reinforce each other. As always, this logic works with varying degrees of intensity. But handling relations with 'social partners' (a revealing term) has become a prime activity of the corporate functions, which have organized, diversified and established hierarchies to cope with this. It is worth noting that the management of HR long bore the marks of egalitarian principles, consisting of treating everyone alike, as far as possible, regardless of the results achieved. Eliminating arbitrary treatment, which in fact means eliminating the discretionary treatment of individuals, in fact amounts to depriving management, and front-line management especially, of real power. Management consequently has no option but to take refuge in technical aspects (where this can still contribute something) or in politics, which sometimes allows one to obtain what one ought not to have to ask for.

Added to this is the fact that power (in some cases symbolic) in companies is also expressed in the terms Stalin used to refer to the pope: how many divisions? This is a question of conquering territories, asserting control over them and ensuring they are 'aligned', which is again achieved by setting rules, procedures and centralizing processes. What remains for the front-line manager in this deluge, along with countless requests for information and statistics each day, not to mention frequent visits from those who want to be able to say they been to see things 'on the ground' for themselves, does not add up to much. He has been swept aside by all these 'intermediate bureaucracies' (see below) that thrive in the complexity they daily contrive to create and in which they alone are capable of giving the impression that they know what they are doing. I am reminded of a major French bank whose top executive wanted to bolster its 'management control' system in order to check that the figures he was receiving were accurate. It was a wise precaution. Every unit and every department frantically set up its own local management control system, each adding its personal touch – an additional metric here, a key ratio there. The result was a disaster. The accumulation of these initiatives taken by bureaucracies scattered across the organization spawned a useless monster that then proved hard to slay. The bank laboured for many years with the resulting millstone around its neck.

But before giving their front-line managers the key role in the campaign to win back control, do companies really trust them? Not that much, as long as this was unnecessary. Are these front-line managers sufficiently distant from the people they are supposed to be overseeing? Does their partial view of the operation allow them to make decisions consistent with the general interest? Perhaps not. Thus, it is best to oversee the overseer and supervise the supervisor. And suddenly the machine races off in the opposite direction, as companies are wont to do, given their unparalleled herd instinct. Companies come to their front-line managers like the Burghers of Calais before the King of England, bearing the keys to the firm on a platter of precious cloth. Now it is up to them. Let them say what they need and it shall be given them. As we shall see, things are not quite so simple in practice.

In this chapter, we will discuss three companies. In the first, we will see how the front-line managers can be 'killed off' once the intermediate bureaucracies have gained their autonomy and enjoy unlimited scope to expand their territory; in the second, we will illustrate how difficult it is to revive the motivation of front-line managers who have been sufficiently burned in the past to be wary of committing themselves again; and in the third we will show that it can be done nevertheless, provided one can overcome the hostility of all those who fear being 'mugged' in the process.

The first case takes us to the branch managers of a bank with an extremely dense nationwide network.[2] Through its branches, the bank had developed an original policy of working closely with its professional clientele, calling on the largest of them daily to collect the day's cheques and so save them a day on their value dates.

The study proved to be a tricky undertaking, for not only did the people supposed to be managing this population (the central HR department) know little about it, it also proved difficult to make contact with the branch managers. The sample of branch managers prepared by the head office staff turned out to contain far from minor errors: some branch managers had left the branch years ago and others had been transferred. In fact, the relevant information was in the hands of their regional managers, who knew these people, and to whom the branch managers referred, but it was certainly not held at the corporate level, which was incapable of updating its database of front-line managers and managers.

Similarly, the branch managers were hard to contact and hence visit: telephone calls went unanswered, no answering machines were available and it proved difficult to make appointments. The initial impression was not exactly that of a responsive, dynamic organization. On the other hand, we quickly gained a sense of a population enjoying broad latitude, particularly in the organization of their day-to-day work. What is more, the mass of directives and demands they received from the higher echelons (regional and the branch network management) – which, themselves being segmented, did not communicate with each other and hence were incapable of prioritizing their own needs – left them considerable room for manoeuvre. As is well known, a silo-type organization at the top means greater discretionary scope for the operational staff.

Solitary dependency

Yet all this counted for little when set against the situation of dependency and extreme solitude of these branch managers and the little real, useful help they received from the other echelons and departments. This sense of 'solitary dependency' came through remarkably clearly in all of the observations recorded.

This population of branch managers was distinguished by its high intellectual and human calibre. Some were higher education graduates and they all displayed a high degree of loyalty and attachment to their firm. For them, grappling with fierce competition, and hence under a continuous obligation to improve labour productivity and service, was perfectly normal. There was widespread agreement on this issue, as summed up in the following testimony:

> *'Before, we talked about quality of service and customer relations. Now, we talk more and more about productivity. We have no choice but to adapt to a continuously changing environment. I do so also because the bank has put its trust me and helped me to get ahead. It's a nice place to work, and one learns a lot here.'*

One could cite many similar enthusiastic testimonials, enough to make top management blush, and yet the most commonly expressed desire of these branch managers was to quit their position as soon as possible, and at any rate not to linger there for too long! Everyone spoke of rapid burnout, a sense of powerlessness, solitude and a lack of resources when it came to performing all those management tasks that had originally attracted them when taking on their responsibilities.

How can we account for this disconnect? What had happened to make these managers, so enthusiastic upon arrival, want to make a swift exit from what had turned out to be a trap? They all condemned the solitude and above all their extreme state of dependency on the higher echelons.

This solitude took the form of a sense of abandonment and incomprehension on the part of the other levels in the bank, and it quickly became clear that the cause of this genuine suffering lay in the management logic put in place by the network. Nit-picking controls, spineless management standards (is one entitled to coffee when taking lunch outside the branch?), a failure to listen when a branch manager raises a genuine problem, etc. – the testimonials speak for themselves:

> *'I'd really like them* [the bosses] *to come and see what goes on. Perhaps it would make them see sense.'*

> *'They really let us down, with no means of doing anything. No one cares about the situation in the branches. In any case, my job is a very solitary one. My boss gives me a bit of information from higher up, she sometimes listens to me, but she doesn't give me much help in solving my problems. We scarcely ever see each other, and we never have a meal together.'*

> *'We communicate only by email with our superiors. We're left on our own. We get no support. If we have a problem, people on leave, we've just got to get on with it.'*

So it was the organization's mode of operation that bred this solitude. With its high degree of formalism, it was 'dehumanized' by its immoderate use of electronic communication, which was so invasive that the recipient could not even tell what was important and what was not. What is more, none of these messages, demands and orders ever touched on the branch managers' problems. One could call this the 'end of the line' syndrome, where everyone else in the organization is busy, launching initiatives and concerned above all with 'covering their backs', but no one really bothers to consider the effects this has on those whose job it is to run the operating units. Those running the operating units understood that no one was interested in their problems and that when they tried to convey them, they were listened to distractedly at best, and at worst they were dismissed as 'constant bellyachers'. Thus, they had developed a genuine sense of being cold-shouldered. This was compounded by the 'multi-divisional dependency' crushing them, which allowed everyone else to externalize all of their bureaucratic 'deviations' on to them, which they gladly did so.

In the first place, the branch managers were dependent on all of the bank's upstream departments, the ones that designed its products to take one example. These departments were made to compete among themselves to ensure priority was given to distributing 'their' products as dynamically as possible, which put endless pressure on the branches. As one branch manager put it:

> *'Each product line is independent and has its own objectives, which serve as a basis for calculating their bonuses. There is a system of internal competition, because our pay itself depends on these products. We even pinch each other's clients between branches. And we have no choice as to the products we market. We're set objectives on the basis of these and I can't refuse. It kills local initiative.'*

This dependence on salespeople was particularly harmful when dealing with the professional client segment, the bank's main target. Sales staff visited these professional clients as often as possible, sometimes daily, in order to pick up their cheques, for example. However, many of these professional clients were small shopkeepers who kept a tight grip on their cash balances. Many of them came to the bank for this service, which was as far as we know unique. But the rest of the organization needed to be capable of backing this up, collecting cheques being just the visible, and no doubt the easiest, portion of the service provided. This was frequently not the case, and in their irritation at not receiving the promised service, customers had only the hapless branch manager at whom to vent their spleen. Yet customers learned fast. They knew which staff member they could count on, and it was to him that they most readily entrusted their high value-added transactions. To the other staff, those who had made promises that were not kept, customers entrusted their simple, routine activities of no great commercial value. This is how a lack of integration within an organization can both doom a promising commercial initiative and 'kill off' the person who is supposed to market it to the client.

The branch manager was responsible for none of these difficulties, although he daily suffered the consequences through dealings with the client. These consequences stemmed from an organization that had been unable – or had not thought or wanted – to adapt its processes to its strategy, and that had shifted the burden of its unwillingness to redraw its traditional segments, management layers and territories on to its lower echelons.

More striking still was the extreme dependence and hence fragility of these managers, even within their own branch. They had little leverage over their staff, being constantly obliged to come to an arrangement with the counter staff, for instance, and to rely on their goodwill, which was given grudgingly. This is what the managers had to say:

> *'They tell me the word "sales" doesn't feature in their job description. I'm constantly trying to figure out how to get them to work. I have the impression I'm talking to a wall.'*

> *'Whenever there's a strike, I have nothing but strikers. They go on strike just to have the day off. It's exhausting! And what am I to do when I've got two people – they're always the same – off sick? I ask for someone to replace them, but I never get anyone.'*

> *'Some of them even refuse to handle sales at the counter! They never say so, of course, even though they signed the "performance letter". What's more, they're supposed to handle customer reception, but they never smile. They're not friendly.'*

Their biggest problems were with the branch staff. To be sure, the work of branch staff was sometimes tedious, with repetitious, time-consuming tasks, and the products they were authorized to sell were unexciting compared with the ones marketed by the real sales staff, those who visited the customers. Another point, and this is a familiar situation, is that the way personnel was managed had little bearing on the actual needs of the branch. It was so tightly planned and bureaucratic that, as one of the branch managers put it: 'To replace a person on sick leave according to the rules, we would have had to foresee and plan for the various illnesses at the start of the year!'

Under those circumstances, what can one expect of staff ensconced in a protective routine from which they have no wish to escape? These counter staff would seize on any excuse to wriggle out of orders or pressures, for which they would expect to receive nothing in return. As a result, they all engaged in a game of 'hide and seek', a lose-lose situation in which the higher echelons failed to provide replacement staff to cope with the endemic absenteeism, while expecting the branch manager to 'shoulder his responsibilities' and deal with his problems himself! But the branch manager, with no means at his disposal, had little choice but to hide behind his badge stating his function and make do as best he could.

Managers and branches were the final link in a chain. Once again, this chain externalized the consequences of its way of doing things to its outer fringes, which were then held to account for the end result vis-à-vis both the client and their own superiors. The latter, meanwhile, acted as a transmission belt for all of the many pressures they came under from all sides: do this, do that, supply information, fill in countless statistical forms, all of which piled up but of which no one outside the branch had any clear idea of the work entailed by this.

Better still, the rhetoric of local management autonomy, of which the bank was very proud, was largely contradicted by its bureaucratic controls and a general lack of trust. Take this 'outburst' from the branch managers:

'They talk all the time about the role of local management, but we are less and less empowered. I can't even send a letter to my clients without having it approved by someone else! They treat us like kids! And they force us to attend pathetic training sessions that are a waste of time.'

'Everything's very hierarchical in this bank. There are the strategists, and the executants. That's us. But we're never consulted about anything. It's all a question of "just get on with it" and "you've got to...". I thought I was going to have more leeway. We're never allowed to take any initiative, or if we are, it's tightly controlled.'

'Being a branch manager is a very tough, physically exhausting job. But you get very little recognition. We get 100 emails a day from all over the place, yet no one realizes it. They tell us: "Anyway, you've got to get it all done." And they never stop telling us we haven't done this or that. One constantly has the feeling of being in the wrong.'

To make up for this, of course, the bank had rummaged through the managerial recipe book and employed a variety of purportedly participatory management tools, including briefings, debriefings and daily reportings, which inevitably drew comparisons with the basic rituals of 'Toyotism'. Yet there again, everything was stereotyped – nothing was integrated or differentiated. The upper management layers saw the network as being there to apply their decisions. This meant that, whatever the needs or customer catchment area, everywhere was treated alike. The same egalitarian principles applied to both clients and personnel.

Even the setting up of platforms to provide the branches with an effective back office and spare them unnecessary work ended up producing the opposite effect. These developed their own autonomy and started issuing standards, procedures and processes reflecting their needs and their pace of work, to which the branches once again were obliged to adapt: doing the branch's housework, the platform's job, itself tended to turn into a headache on a daily basis.

'Victimhood'

In other words, whichever way one looked at things, the story was always the same: intermediate bureaucracies, wrapped up in their own concerns, made a lot of noise, held meetings, did some thinking and then externalized on to defenceless front-line units the results of their activity; that activity was virtual in terms of its utility, but all-devouring in its consequences.

It is no exaggeration to say that, caught between these irresponsible (in the true sense of the word) management layers and personnel over whom they had no real power to manage, the front-line managers were literally crushed, which explains why they were in such a hurry to put an end to such an untenable situation.

Our task now was to examine the strategies deployed by front-line managers in order to cope with such difficult circumstances. The first, not surprisingly, was to withdraw into themselves. A not inconsiderable proportion of this group, the most active, the most dynamic and hence most readily redeployable, looked around for alternative employment elsewhere. For them, a stint with the bank represented an additional line on their CV. For the bank, this was a clear loss. It simply served as a training course for personnel worth keeping, but who were quick to move on.

For the remainder, the majority, this withdrawal took the form of sitting back and giving up the fight in the face of overwhelming circumstances. They were easy to spot: they would be welcoming, saying that everything was fine, that there were no problems and that the staff were motivated and competent. Then, as the conversation wore on, things quickly became clear and the interviewee finished by listing all of the difficulties described above. These people had presumably tried to institute what they considered appropriate working practices, but had then come into conflict with the staff and their trade unions, at which point their superiors expressed disapproval and distanced themselves from the situation. They would not be caught out like this again.

A second strategy consisted of compensating for the absence of any real power by by employing a closer, more friendly management style in relation to their staff. This involved creating an 'atmosphere', a 'consensus', in order to secure personnel's acquiescence when these were the only tools available. This represented a strategy of accentuation, as it were, to quote a notion that will crop up later. The people concerned described it thus:

> *'My superiors don't think I'm sufficiently authoritarian and ask me why I don't apply more sanctions. But I can get my way through diplomacy. At least there's a good atmosphere in the branch.'*

> *'I try to find solutions to get results, but I prefer non-stressful management methods. It's the old-style approach to management: I set the example, I communicate a lot, I seek consensus and support for my decisions. It's a very tough branch with a strong union tradition. I myself am a union member. I never try to force things through.'*

To be frank, this was a conservative strategy, based on a tacit agreement to leave everything as it was, especially acquired rights, both official and unofficial. It drove the organization's endogenous tendencies to extremes, and these were exacerbated daily by personnel and the hierarchy, acting in tandem instead of counterbalancing each other. It set in stone, as it were, the front-line managers' acceptance of their situation of dependency and isolation. However, in so doing, it sent a clear message that one could not simply ask these managers to go from a situation of victimhood to a dynamic and enthusiastic commitment purely on the grounds that the environment had changed. The following case will demonstrate this.

*

In the next case study, the question facing a large retailer[3] was to find out how hard it would be to transfer to the store managers a responsibility hitherto wielded by 'organizers' dependent on one of the corporate divisions. Until now, these people had the job of 'reorganizing'

the stores, as the need arose, and of reassigning employees in accordance with the new configuration. As a result, they possessed knowledge (the data serving to calculate a store's yield) and know-how (the
ability to interpret those data). The project was part of a wider process
of rationalizing the employees' work and boosting productivity, based
on the assumption that responsibility for configuring the stores could
gradually be shifted to the local management. Here again, as soon as
the question turned to trying to get more out of employees, the natural tendency was to shift the burden on to the front-line managers.
The senior managers feared that these organizers would be reluctant
to transfer to other people an activity that gave them a measure
of power, since fitting out shops and assigning people accordingly
implied defining job descriptions and tasks of varying degrees of desir-
ability, and hence an unofficial hierarchy among the staff.

   It quickly became apparent that the reorganization process had
gradually turned into a routine. It took place every two or three years
and was very well accepted by the employees, who feared the mission of the organizer (if executed in accordance with the principles
laid down by the top management) more than the organizer himself.
The latter had long grasped that the best way to deal with the staff
was to come to an arrangement with them, enabling the organizer
to wield power without running the risk of conflict with this group
of people, given the sensitive nature of labour relations with potentially adverse consequences for him. Some employees openly said
that (past) reorganizations had been based on 'the colour of a person's hair' (i.e., on seniority), thus indicating that equal weight had
been given to the employee's personal situation as to the economic
rationale behind the revamp. One can see why the top management
harboured some misgivings as to whether they would be able to
relinquish this discretionary power!

   Yet our analysis revealed something different, namely that the
problems involved in modernizing the management of these stores
had more to do with the capacity of local managers to shoulder
this responsibility than with the organizers' reluctance (which was
easily overcome) to transfer all or part of their knowledge to the local
managers.

   This observation deserves to be qualified. There was a fringe of
younger managers, with prior experience in frequently tougher environments, who were irritated (or worse) by the employees' now

over-protected situation, and who were calling for something different. Here is what one said, a little brutally:

> *'I wanted to join a firm where they took care of the personnel. But this was too much! We manage our personnel like schoolkids. Not enough rigour and severity. We could be more efficient while still treating people well. Serious cases of professional misconduct go unpunished. This isn't a rehabilitation centre or a social assistance centre. In fact, they aren't afraid of anything, since they've never seen anyone fired. We don't respect the Labour Code, which would let us take appropriate disciplinary measures. It's annoying, and it has a cost.'*

What this expert expressed is that some managers were indeed ready to take effective responsibility for the stores. However, above all it showed that, for the moment at least, they did not have the support of their superiors to embark on a different policy. Clearly this is a widespread syndrome!

Power without responsibility, responsibility without power

Let us take a closer look at the workings of this local system, which 'optimized' its labour relations dimension at the expense of economic efficiency. This featured a sharp distinction between employees (the labour relations aspect) and the store's configuration (the economic aspect). It was accepted as a given that the same person could not have handled both aspects (why not?) and that the layout of these stores demanded know-how and experience that their managers were not supposed to have (really?). Managing the former (the employees) was the task of the store managers, while the organizers handled the other aspect (store layout). All this was commonly agreed without undue discussion. Thus, we were dealing here with an accepted 'unspoken hierarchy', based on the supposed difficulty of the different tasks, managing people doubtless being assumed to be easier than managing technical aspects.

In fact, as we shall see, the separation between the employees and the store configuration had another function within this system, one that was the opposite of what has just been described. It maintained the balance between the general satisfaction of all of the actors, who have taken on board the notion that, de facto, the labour relations aspect prevailed over the economic outcome. All of the actors concerned therefore saw to it that no one was penalized by the actions of the others, thus keeping this way of doing things remarkably stable.

Undoubtedly, though, the organizer was the dominant player, since he controlled what was crucial to the employee, namely his assignment. By shouldering responsibility for what could prove to be tricky decisions, the organizer spared the manager the risk of damaging his labour relations. In other words, this was an original system in which one actor (the organizer) wielded power without responsibility and the other (the store manager) responsibility without power.

The significant power wielded by the organizer clearly emerged in the satisfaction he expressed at doing his job, emphasizing how interesting it was, the autonomy he enjoyed and the variety:

'We have deadlines, obviously, but we also have a lot of freedom in managing our timetable.'

'Provided the work is done on time, there's no problem with the higher ups. We are very free to manage our time. We work like experts, which is what we ought to be, in fact.'

'It's comfortable. I'm not stressed the way I was when I was a department supervisor. We're sheltered from the customers and personnel management problems. That's a fantastic relief. I like this functional job.'

Two things emerged from this: first, that these organizers felt better off for having no operational responsibility. That is why they emphasized the notion of expertise, which means they had more of a 'support' function than a direct responsibility. As regards the initial question, this already suggested significant latitude for negotiation as to a possible change in the position of these people. Secondly, they were very well aware of the far greater difficulty of the manager's role. Their own comfort and that of the manager (to a lesser degree) depended on coming to an arrangement with the employees so as to limit the occasions for conflict with them. Needless to say, the organizer insisted at every opportunity on the need to comply with the rules and to respect economic considerations. However, in so doing, he sent a clear message to the other actors: no pressure, please, otherwise the rules will have to be applied strictly. One organizer put this point subtly:

> 'The organizer is a cause of anxiety to the employees. They think things may go badly and that everything's been decided in advance. But that's not true. There's no pressure on me, either from above or from below. I'm simply the guardian of the Highway Code. But the main thing is for employees to feel at ease in their work.'

Needless to say, in the practical and daily performance of his work, the organizer placed the main emphasis on 'accompanying', that special moment when he formed a close relationship with the employee, who explained to him the difficulties of his job or how customer behaviour was changing. This was when the organizer gathered the living information which, according to him, could neither be described nor summarized, nor, above all, condensed into a computer program. This was where his 'know-how' (which was probably over-estimated) lay, allowing him to interpret the data thus compiled. Consequently, as we observed in the embassies earlier, the organizers had consistently refused, or rendered useless, the tools made available to them.

However, it was also during this face-to-face meeting with the employee that the organizer negotiated what was acceptable and what was not (which in fact concerned reassignments) and that he came to an arrangement that benefited everyone. Not that there were never any clashes or that everyone came away content, but this remained marginal. Here are the words of another organizer:

> 'I know all the employees in my stores and I have good relations with them. But there are positions to be axed, and it sometimes happens that we change their working habits. In this store, for example, out of about 50 staff there are three who have stopped saying hello to me. But I'm on good terms with all the others, and in any case, I'm not paid to make friends.'

The end product of this process, of this 'revamp', had to be presented, explained and sometimes justified to the employees concerned. In reality, it was the organizer who handled this presentation and took responsibility for the decisions taken, to the huge relief of the store's manager. Needless to say, the latter was the 'project leader'. It was he, after all, who would have to implement the decisions taken and who was supposed to exercise his authority over his subordinates. But during the presentation he saw the organizer's presence and involvement as a vital asset for himself. There is no ambiguity in what this manager had to say:

> *'The organizers are increasingly going to become technicians, advisers. I think that's a good thing. <u>But</u> [emphasis added], they mustn't lose their links with the employees. They mustn't become out of touch with the people on the ground. I can piece the data together, but they've got to be reliable. But when you do it all yourself, you're liable to pollute your own data. You need an outsider to take part.'*

This is a direct expression of the very strong dependence of the store managers on the organizers. So why were they so fearful of taking on additional responsibilities? They argued, and the organizers agreed, that it was a question of a lack of time. True, the managers did work a great deal, their 'over-working' being the adjustment variable that let them cope with their tasks. It is true, too, that they were answerable to a hierarchy that provided little help but demanded a lot from them, including statistics, reports and information that could surely be collected by other means. Therefore, the reasons for their withdrawal must be sought elsewhere.

These managers were accountable for the results of their store in both financial and quality of service terms, the latter of which was now a discriminating factor in this crowded business. At the same time, they had very few 'managerial' levers in their hands at present and all their efforts were focused on managing their human resources – in fact, dealing with absenteeism, which was a sizeable issue in these demanding activities. Their obsession was with leaving no section 'untended'. This implied obtaining a flexible attitude from their staff, which needed to be bargained for. But they had little to offer in exchange, as this manager pointed out:

> *'One needs to tread carefully with the staff, [to] be careful what you say. You need to keep an eye on the climate and do nothing to make things worse, otherwise you'll get nothing, and we don't have much to give them. You have to show we understand their problems and difficulties.'*

It is now possible to understand the difficulty facing the Executive Committee: it wanted to 'empower' its store managers. Fair enough. In order to do so, it planned to give them 'power', i.e., something they could control with respect to the population they were supposed to manage. Fair enough again. But in proceeding with our analysis, it became clear that they were not ready to take on this new area, i.e., reorganization, with its potential to aggravate labour relations. In other words, this is an interesting question of a systemic nature, i.e., how can sufficient distance be placed between store managers and their staff so as to balance their now predominantly labour relations logic with the increased importance of economic criteria? We find here that the initial assumption, namely that the organizers were reluctant to transfer their activity to the managers, was misleading. The right assumption concerned the capacity of the managers to change their game, which was risky for them. This capacity does not depend on 'them', as one hears daily in companies trying to shift the systemic complexities they are unable or unwilling to deal with on to individuals. It depends on the behaviour of their superiors, who have left them alone until now, and who now see that the organizers' withdrawal leaves a void they would be incapable of filling. In a word, they are being offered both increased responsibilities and solitude.

Clearly, if the store manager was going to be obliged to deal single-handed with this new relationship with employees, in unfamiliar conditions where economic concerns took priority over labour relations, and if all were agreed to consider this as 'his problem' and that the rest of the organization was there merely to observe, measure and judge, then failure was inevitable. Yet, during the interviews, the upper echelons never conveyed the impression that they were fully involved in the change of trajectory planned for the store managers. They observed what was happening 'from afar', even though they alone were in a position to relieve these store managers of their obsession with labour relations.

The first need was to show the store managers that the climate of labour relations – in this case, absenteeism and the frequency of disputes – was not the paramount criterion for evaluating them. It is not enough to state this; one needs to demonstrate it. Ronald Reagan did it with the air traffic controllers; Georges Besse put it into practice at Renault. It is far from easy, because it implies working to ensure that disputes remain the exception and accepting them as a potential cost of implementing change. Here it was the upper echelons, above all, that had some learning to do. But they also had to learn to give up their arm's length stance vis-à-vis the stores and become actors in their change. There was no miracle solution to this: it implied reviewing the process of evaluation, promotion and compensation right across the board, to make them jointly responsible for the results achieved, rather than this being solely the responsibility of those doing the measuring. As we can see, winning back the front-line managers implies asserting control over the intermediate bureaucracies first.

The intermediate bureaucracies

In the third case, drawn from a large manufacturer of precision instruments,[4] we will observe the strategies deployed by these intermediate bureaucracies to delay or thwart a project aimed at transferring the bulk of power to the operators on the shop floor and their front-line managers. Even though the company couched its initial question in terms of the 'values' of these middle-rank executives (plant department managers), this was really a question of a loss of real power. The hostility displayed by the employee categories concerned cannot therefore be put down to some kind of 'resistance to change', a notion as vague as it is empty, but rather reflects a sensible defence of their own interests. This is not only a more realistic way of formulating the problem but also helps to avoid needlessly arousing feelings of guilt or playing the blame game. It preserves the future, in case these populations would one day be obliged to find their place in a different operational format. To understand that this is strategic behaviour and not 'narrow-mindedness' is to avoid human wastage.

The resulting plan was designed to secure the greater involvement of the operators on the ground and their front-line managers (instructors and unit supervisors), who had hitherto been confined to passively taking orders from above. At the time of carrying out this study, the operation was genuinely successful. The actors displayed remarkable maturity: not only did they 'commit' themselves to quality and 'continuous improvement' (to use the language of Toyotism) but they also understood the direct connection between their performance and their site's capacity to survive, having been under threat for a while. Even their criticism of the constant inflation in the number of indicators of all kinds and of the ever-greater length of time spent at the computer did not diminish their commitment. Like good students, they spontaneously described their 'rituals', emphasized the need to 'speak up' and, when asked about possible further improvements, said that since the progress was continuous, there was always room for improvement! They had signed up to the foundations of Toyotism, including its rhetoric. In fact, three factors came together here to explain this 'grassroots' commitment to 'continuous improvement'.

First, there was the matter of the survival instinct: the approach held out the hope of preserving their jobs and of a level playing field in confronting foreign competition. They evinced a surprising knowledge of economic facts on occasion, enabling them to continuously compare their performance with that of other firms in the sector.

The second reason for their unqualified support for the system would delight the fiercest critics of Taylorism: this proposed approach reinjected meaning into their work or, looking a little deeper, it let them think about the meaning of work. Their comments were edifying:

> '*I like it here, because one's constantly having to see what comes next. That's good.*'

> '*We're chalking up amazing scores without stretching ourselves too much, thanks to the continuous improvements.*'

> '*At last we've stopped working like idiots. That's why everyone's smiling and chatting when they turn up in the morning.*'

It is important not to take this too much at face value or to see a brave new world in this, but a win-win situation had plainly emerged between the company and its grassroots units. This also explained why the front-line managers were overloaded with work to the point where they were spontaneously working longer hours. There was no sense that they were fed up, with the exception mentioned above of the number of indicators they were obliged to supply. In a way, everyone was eagerly awaiting the next stage.

Finally, the third reason was that the deployment of this plan entailed a genuine transfer of power from the top down, or at least a redefinition of these power relationships: managers were going to have to relinquish their traditional hierarchical stance and adopt a more approachable, attentive posture if they wanted to remain players. Indeed, the operatives on the ground had precise expectations of them: they wanted them to 'bring in work', to go out and sign up new orders, and they expected their direct supervisors to sort out their daily difficulties. They almost seemed to be suggesting a new distribution of roles where, regardless of one's position in the hierarchy, legitimacy comes from one's performance and skills, not from one's status.

This is where things became complicated. As foreseen by the plan's instigators, the difficulties came from the more senior executives, both those on-site and those at head office, who looked askance at this transfer. At the most obvious (though also the most superficial) level, their objections were couched in terms of 'values' and 'culture'. Given their early training and habits rooted in decades of experience, these executives would find it hard to start acting differently. Admittedly, they were not interested in the methodical repetition of gestures or in the importance of 'rituals'. They were interested in exploits, the exceptional, what is different, and the ability to 'get things done'. 'They each want to invent their own thing', said one operator with a grin. Priority was given to conceptual activities, which were meant to be as sophisticated and intellectual as possible. Execution and production were of secondary importance and could be delegated to others, being devoid of nobility, on the understanding that what was decided would come to pass.

An example of the system effect

All of the above is true but represents only the visible tip of the iceberg. This is because the executives lost both power and autonomy in this adventure: their hierarchical power and the autonomy that came with segmented departments. In interviews with them, all of the executives spontaneously emphasized all of the constraints that could diminish the opportunities for them to play a part in the plan. Naturally, the first of the constraints was a question of budgets: we'd like to, but we don't have the resources! In addition, we must boost productivity at all costs and quickly. A production manager put it emphatically:

> *'We are continually hounded by productivity. Don't forget that, whatever happens, because people get the impression the message has changed and*

that we're moving backwards. They stress quality and that's good. But budgetary pressures quickly bring you back into line. And then it's up to us to get the job done!'

The second constraint related to the growing and ever more time-consuming demands from head office. As one site executive put it:

'They're constantly demanding more and more. We've no idea what it's used for, but presumably they've got to keep the machine going. But we too know how to send out smokescreens and mix things up.'

Now we have all the necessary pieces of the jigsaw puzzle to understand the emerging 'system effect' which could hinder the plan's success: to compensate for a real loss of their hierarchical power, the site executives invoked a host of external constraints on the production process, with a tendency to exaggerate their importance. The head office executives had de facto encouraged this strategy, having no intention of being stripped of their power via an approach that prioritized production and the grassroots operators. To 'thwart' this process, they had constantly stepped up their demands for indicators, objectives and data, useful or otherwise. The on-site executives had used this to bolster their role as a 'shield' on the shop floor, and more generally their power, which they derived from the 'information differential' in their favour. In other words, the increasingly bureaucratic nature of the plan, something vehemently denounced by the operatives and their front-line managers, was a useful resource for the on-site executives in managing their own troops. And it was not the least of the paradoxes surrounding this situation that it had given rise to this de facto alliance between the on-site executives and those at head office, two groups that were at loggerheads in the traditional system, including in terms of what they had to say about each other. We can now see clearly just how harmful these intermediate bureaucracies can be, making matters all the more complicated when they have only a small stake in the chaos resulting from this artificial complexity. This is most fully expressed in the invasion of 'processes'. The next chapter looks at this powerful, disturbing trend.

5
Integration and Processes: A Marriage Made in Hell

I noted in the Introduction to this book the temptation experienced by companies that feel they have lost control to regain that control by introducing processes of all kinds. These processes are supposed to guarantee not only that everything is being done the same way everywhere, but also that everything is done as it should be. I pointed out that this response was reminiscent of administrative thinking, the outcomes of which are open to question. I will try now to go further and show that not only does this not work, but that it actually breeds confusion and, to use the companies' own language, it destroys more value than it creates.

Let me be clear: I am not criticizing companies for seeking to organize what they do more effectively or even for trying to assert control over what they do. They are right to set rules, procedures, indicators and processes. Indeed, there can be no collective action without some rules, explicit or otherwise. A constant feature of the games of Ancient Rome was to set people against each other on the basis of brute force alone; both the gladiators of yesterday and today's sportsmen and women have invented at least a minimum number of rules to organize their contests.

As far as companies are concerned, the issue is how they do so and the consequences this has on the way in which they function, and in particular on the 'commitment' of their members, so widely regarded as one of the 'keys to success'.

The problem for these companies is to control what they are responsible for and to explain to actors how they should do what they are supposed to do. In order to achieve this, they institute benchmarks based on best practice, call in consultants specializing in 'organizational design' and processes, and they end up with a theoretical chart showing what ought to be, leaving it up to the actors to make it so. If things do not work out, then it is the fault of someone else, of those whose job it was to execute the design who, for whatever reasons, failed to do things the way they were told to do them. Yet we have long known that, of the three classic phases of a change process – understanding the problem, framing solutions and implementing them – it is the third that is by far the hardest to achieve. This explains why most senior managers keep the second phase – the easiest – for themselves and always subcontract out the third phase and its associated uncertainties. This is only human and it is part of the daily life of organizations.

The myth of clarity

The most embarrassing thing about the situation described above is the faulty reasoning behind this focus on processes: there is a myth of clarity in companies that is akin to the calls for transparency now being heard in all sectors of our societies. We do know that behind this frantic search for clarity (at least in what other people are doing) is the need all actors feel to reduce the uncertainty surrounding them. This need also explains why, however uncertain the world may be, top managers are always expected to have a 'clear strategy', not because it is the right one but because it gives a sense of security to all those fearful of the unpredictability the future brings.

However, as soon as emphasis is placed on homogeneity and clarity – the Siamese twins of modern management – it is necessary to find ways to achieve them. This is where rules, procedures, processes, indicators and reporting in all its forms come in.

As sociologists would say, everyone thinks – or pretends to think – that the rule defines the game, that the actors apply in a linear fashion what they are asked to apply and use their intelligence solely to comply with what is asked of them. This explains the frantic proliferation of processes, on whose production our celebrated intermediate bureaucracies thrive. The most surprising thing for the observer is how earnestly everyone pretends to believe in them. There is a consensus around creating these processes (this single word will suffice in covering all of the different processes enumerated above) in order to define each task with precision. Whether or not the actors apply and, needless to say, use these processes 'strategically' is nobody's concern, especially not of those who issue them. I recall the head of one large food services company who called me in one day to tell me that a major consultancy had designed a perfect organization for him, but that he had no idea how to make it work. Children will only show an interest in even the most splendid and sophisticated electric trains if they actually work.

So why is all this so hard to execute? Because the rules do not define the game: they structure it. This somewhat crude remark conceals a simple fact of life that everyone both understands and overlooks, namely that rules are important not because of what they say but because of what the actors make of them.[1] I shall refrain from referring to the often-cited example of air traffic controllers, whose freedom and bargaining power is augmented by the fact that air traffic is organized by so many rules as to be inapplicable, which makes it dependent on the controllers' goodwill in order to keep the planes flying. The French State Audit Court has shown all the benefits the controllers derive from this absurd situation. One could also cite the absurdities that flow from the strict application of the precautionary principle.[2] More generally, this positive 'passion for procedures' now (once again!) pervading companies is creating neither order, harmony nor predictability. It gives all of the actors concerned considerable latitude. No one can criticize them for using it, since all they are doing when they 'beat the system' is to underline the inconsistencies and contradictions in what they are asked to do. Consequently, to keep 'things working' regardless, the actors will have to select, adapt, transform and on occasion wear themselves out even, as we shall see in one exceptional case.[3]

What we have here is the reverse of the desired effect, and it takes time (and often disasters) for companies to wake up to the fact or agree to lift the veil on what everyone knew and tacitly acquiesced in. In place of harmony (integration), we find a proliferation of parochial politics, with everyone devising their own means to ensure things work nevertheless. Each actor reinvents the wheel, and all we can do is hope they all reinvent the same wheel in order to achieve the desired integration. In fact, this is frequently what happens.

It is worth noting that companies are especially careful to distinguish between integration – where everyone follows the same processes – and centralization – where everything is decided at the top level. This is an interesting intellectual distinction, which has its appeal, spawning internal memos to explain and demonstrate how things should be carried out. However, the outcome is the same. Indeed, we would be hard put to explain why decisions taken at the top level on the one hand and the fact that everyone follows identical processes on the other hand should yield different results. Above all, this is a form of rhetoric aimed at reassuring those who see integration as a threat to their autonomy. As we saw in the earlier chapters, they can stand up for themselves. In Part III, we shall see that some firms have long understood – and many have followed in their footsteps – that fuzziness is more conducive than clarity to control; that all of these processes generate difficulties more than they create visibility; and that instead of giving companies the means to regain control over themselves, the processes discourage those with good intentions and encourage routine, bureaucratic behaviour.

There may be something even more serious than this faulty reasoning: in what follows, we will observe a handful of companies in the process of 'professionalization'. This is the polite term used to signal one's intention to replace the actors' initiative (their 'entrepreneurship') with 'more rational' management methods via those processes and reporting systems we have been talking about. Management rhetoric presents the transition as a normal phase in the company's growth (as we shall see, it is nothing of the sort). But the individuals concerned regard it as a sign of mistrust. No matter how it is explained to them that this is not the case (fortunately), in their eyes it discredits the tandem comprised of smooth functioning thanks to their goodwill and autonomy vis-à-vis their superiors.

Some companies get round this by explaining to their employees that this standardization has been demanded by outside regulators or 'certifiers'. This is both true and false – true, because the life of companies is permeated by these certification norms and safety standards that allow some of their issuers to cover themselves in the event of a problem, and others to scoop up whatever golden eggs the goose happens to lay, and false, because, in the final analysis, the regulators' reasoning is exactly the same as the preceding one, which we have just shown to be in vain. To conclude, achieving a quality standard may earn a company certification, but it is no guarantee of quality. Sometimes, too, the norm can help make operators aware of the importance of mastering certain gestures and the necessity of repeating them. More generally though, the transition to (over-) rationalized forms of work (and usually there is no one in charge of the machine that churns them out) destroys the initial trust so vital in resolving what no norm or standard will ever resolve.

The difficulties of integration

Two initial company case studies will bring to life the difficulties encountered in this march towards integration and professionalization.

The first company manufactured convenience goods. Having achieved outstanding growth under its late founder, the firm went on an acquisition spree, both in its home country and abroad, progressively capturing a significant slice of the global market. During its period of conquest, its natural focus was on 'countries', where business was done, and on the business lines where the products were designed. At the time of our study, management was considering overhauling this organizational concept. As such, it was in a state of transition.[4]

On the whole, employees saw the company as a place where life was pleasant, when individuals were respected and its executives were 'motivated', thanks to its universally acknowledged dynamism and innovative capacities. Great importance was attached to 'human problems', which meant that people – in the words of the company – were seen as the keys to success. Lastly, everyone appreciated the ease of dealing with each other, including with the members of the Executive Committee, whom anyone could contact as needed. Sometimes, emphasizing the 'human' aspect provokes emotional reactions that come as a shock to advocates of a more professional management style. But this was unquestionably a worker-friendly, consensual environment, and actors appreciated it all the more when they compared it with what they saw in other companies. This was a 'company built on trust', and this trust[5] was a form of 'capital' on which the company had hitherto relied and viewed as a key to its success.

But change was in the air: the organization felt itself to be 'in transition', although no one was able to say clearly what the end point of this transition would be. But we know from experience that one does not need to know where one is going in order to get there! On closer examination, however, it became clear that the company was in transition from a predominantly 'entrepreneurship' model to a new, 'company' model, in the sense of an integrated company. For the managers, this was a precondition of growth and of the success of its acquisitions in particular. Needless to say, this process was accompanied by a far-reaching redistribution of power, with winners and losers: henceforth priority was to go to the business lines, which were to be the focal points for 'integration' in terms of their responsibility for the design and execution of 'product' strategy. This was being done to the detriment of the 'brands' and 'markets', and went hand in hand with the institution of processes, procedures and reporting channels, all signalling the company's 'professionalization'. These were supposed to enable it, in theory at least, to develop a clear strategy and control its execution. The practical outcomes were very different.

The first and most visible consequence was the emergence of a group of people more focused on products than on customers. This is a characteristic we observe as soon as a company starts thinking that its brands 'create' the market rather than having to adapt to it. This is the way part of the cosmetics industry functions. In the case before us here, the choice had been made to develop products far from their markets, the latter being expected to sell these without over-emphasizing their specific characteristics. This raised no major problems as long as the places of design and production were located within these markets (in Europe, for example). But once the company began 'going global', the fact that product design remained in the original production sites automatically widened the distance between what was being designed and local demand. The priority enjoyed by products over markets increasingly became a handicap. The question now was how to find the means to impose this. One of our informants described the situation as follows:

'For very many years, we imposed European products, because that's where the volume production was. And we are still very European. Of course, we have tried to get a handle on local needs, and there are a few positive examples. But we are far, very far from our goal. And even if we do sometimes manage to get our message across, we are very slow in executing and bringing out products. That's because our

development processes are so cumbersome, because of the number of
people involved, and the fact that all decisions have to be referred to
the top.'

This comment from the markets merely expressed their own interests, after all. But the people on the industrial side, who had less of a
stake in this issue, said roughly the same thing:

'Our Group is product-driven. There's no doubt about it. In our meetings
to discuss our "product business lines", we talk product, we never talk
customer. The customer only gets a look into the company when some-
thing negative happens. Otherwise, he doesn't count for much.'

One can see why the business lines, to which power had been given,
established their autonomy relative to the rest of the company. To
use management-speak, it could be said that this was the outcome
of a poorly understood matrix mode of operation, which tipped the
organization in one direction with no real counterweight to balance
it. Neither the markets nor the production people were able to assert
themselves vis-à-vis the business lines. It is worth noting, in passing,
the way in which certain modes of operation crop up over and over
again: once more, it was the operational workers in the business
lines, those who designed the products and hence exercised power
in reality, who asserted their autonomy. They functioned in silos,
making no real attempt to work collectively and ensure that the staff
functions (HR and finance, for example) did not attempt to integrate
them. To complete the circle, unsurprisingly as we shall see later,
head office was striving to compensate for this undivided power of
the business lines by producing ever more sophisticated and detailed
procedures and controls. In a word, the organization's product focus
generated bureaucratic forms of control, and it is worth pondering
their effects. Like facts, system effects can be stubborn.

When integration widens the gap between actors

Integration via the business lines was of course a problem for the
markets, since it ran counter to the traditional autonomy of the
local actors and their commitment to the aforementioned 'entrepreneurial' model. In addition, their loss of autonomy and power was

not confined to product development. Other aspects of their responsibilities were starting to slip from their grasp, namely aspects of purchasing and sales, which were traditional areas of local freedom in organizations not yet highly integrated. A 'large accounts' manager was very clearsighted in his description of the change:

'Until now, the countries still had one thing: sales. But with the arrival of international clients, they set up central purchasing organizations that selected their suppliers for strategic products. The result for the countries: I handle prices and references for ten countries with one of my staff. I negotiate in place of the countries, who don't like it, obviously.'

Meanwhile, the countries were in total disarray and expressed this:

'I'm not very clear what my room for manoeuvre is. I don't know anymore if I can decide this or that. In any case, when Europe takes a decision, they don't pay any attention to the role of the markets. They sometimes even send us people who don't speak the language, or for certain products their customer support service is in another country.'

'No allowance is ever made for the specific features of our market, and I can tell you one of our brands has suffered from this for some years. The development people in Europe aren't open-minded, and they're not inclined to listen to us. There's a lot of hard work to do.'

It is no minor paradox to note that this attempted integration widened the gap between actors. It is easy to see why, because the business lines seemed so indifferent to the problems their approach could cause for others. To put it another way, the product development sphere was perfectly happy to reproduce the mode of operation inherited from the days when the company was focused on Europe. This widened the gulf between actors, their perceptions diverged and the different levels of the organization came to distrust each other. One 'product development' project leader had this criticism to make of the countries:

'The subsidiaries want to do things on their own. They're really mistrustful. And that's a source of problems. They come to us when their project's all done and dusted, and then they pretend to ask our opinion.'

When the same interviewee described those taking part in a product development decision, the list was not long:

> '*Once a month, product development committees meet with the activity's boss, the marketing boss, and those working on the product. They're the ones that decide. And it's very difficult for a country to request a product. That's because they don't really know ... it's local ... nobody knows.*'

Finally, the only suggestion the product developers had in response to the company's global expansion was not to delocalize all or part of the product design, but rather to import non-European skills where needed. As such, the company's attempts to forge greater professionalism while keeping power distributed very locally accentuated the trend towards fragmentation rather than integration (for the moment), creating an organization more conducive to partisanship than to consistency. This fragmentation was further reinforced by the 'riposte' dreamed up the company, which led to the emergence of an increasing tendency towards bureaucracy in its methods of operation. This tendency, as we have observed already, is inherent in the fact of giving priority to products, which is responsible for the endogenous character of the organization.

Everything is controlled; nothing is controlled

However, it may seem curious, provocative even, to speak of bureaucracy when talking about a company like this, whose image is the reverse of what this word usually evokes. But I use bureaucracy here in its sociological meaning, in the sense that priority is given to internal questions (reporting, procedures, decision-making processes) over the demands of the market (real or supposed). And the fact is that the cumbersome nature of the reporting system was as apparent to those subject to it as to those who designed it (the corporate staff in the finance function). This is how a member of the former category described it:

> '*The corporate people are making increasing demands, placing a growing burden on us and preventing us from getting on with our sales work. I've nothing against it ... but, well ... everyone wants his report... I'd rather they didn't ask us for the same thing over and over.*'

A member of the latter category echoed this complaint:

> *'The company's reporting process is very cumbersome, and even so it isn't comprehensive, where cash is concerned, for example. I'd been hoping that would change, but despite our new system, I can't see anything coming. In fact, management want to know everything and are endlessly demanding more and more inessential details.'*

This came as no surprise. We are dealing here with a very classical (and contemporary) attempt at integration through processes, with financial and sales reporting as the backbone. That line managers in the countries should complain about this is perfectly normal. These processes are part of the puzzle that is progressively encroaching on their autonomy. More striking was the 'shared angle of view' uniting everyone in their exasperation at the resulting 'micro-management'. Once the machine is on the rails, nothing can stop it, as if the possibilities afforded by these new practices were a licence to go everywhere, know everything and control everything. Grafted onto a traditional 'culture' of taking care of the details, yesterday's virtue becomes today's vice. How can a firm double in size, embark on a global strategy and preserve the habits of a large small or medium enterprise? Those amongst its staff who lay claim to this culture of detail, feeding it by means of ever more numerous and sophisticated processes, are also the people driving the organization's 'professionalization'. This presupposes both greater delegation and increased cooperation among senior managers, so as to avoid the bottlenecks created by their pusillanimous micro-management. Failure to connect these different factors, i.e., the lack of a systemic vision of the organization, traps them within the vicious circle of ineffectual control, which itself breeds a rising tide of demands that merely pile up rather that complement each other: everything is controlled, but nothing is controlled. Two recent recruits (thanks to expansion) expressed their surprise at this:

> *'I'm used to matrix organizations, and anyway, there is no other model. What surprised me was the very strong involvement of top management and the lack of delegation. I wonder how one can manage growth with so little delegation. Here we simultaneously have very close involvement by senior managers in micro-details, and an absence of real control, which means that important issues are not dealt with.'*

'Here, they're steering an aircraft carrier like a bicycle! Every week we're required to report sales forecasts up to the Executive Committee. It's a lack of trust and the sign they're genuinely worried. The top managers are drowning beneath a flood of useless information, which means decisions aren't being made. Or else they are done so brutally and in the absence of any criteria. It's becoming haphazard.'

One could hardly better describe this logic of panic resulting in painstaking but ineffectual controls. Added to this was poor integration at the summit – hardly surprisingly – with each senior manager embarking on his own projects, each of which naturally took precedence over the others. Following a well-known process, the resulting logjams gave the lower ranks greater room for manoeuvre, allowing them to establish their own priorities where their superiors had failed to do so. The wheel was about to come full circle: the company's de facto centralization hindered the emergence of a local management with sufficient autonomy to take initiatives. Everything was referred upwards, to the business lines or to top management, which were then submerged under a welter of tasks, reports, information and decisions to be taken. Senior managers replied to all of these haphazardly or, at least, that was how the rest of the organizations perceived things.

Indeed, this accounted for the slowness of the decision-making process. Logjams were not the only cause, but the situation was compounded by the strategy of integration – in reality, of centralization – and by the processes. The natural cost of all this was poor responsiveness, as denounced by one executive:

'What we really feel is holding us back are the lead times, which are slowing us down. For example, they want everyone to apply the same recruitment strategy. But that creates bottlenecks. We lose the good ones when they're in a hurry.'

In other words, this organization was consistent with itself. Even if, I repeat, it was in a state of transition (it might be worth considering again at this point what the end point of this transition was intended to be), it had made a series of non-choices or contradictory choices. It thought 'professionalization' meant control and that this was obtained via a plethora of rules of procedures. Yet, at the same time, its top managers refused to relax their grip, and in the resulting confusion actors had a choice of either 'going missing' and taking refuge in withdrawal and apathy, thereby 'destroying value', or manipulating (in the sociological sense) a system now completely out of control to their own advantage. Either way, it was a failure.

This 'control freakery' can go further still. Let us look at the case of a company that built large-scale plants requiring major capital expenditures in the Middle East. It was organized into project teams, and what prompted the study in question[6] was a sense of malaise among the 'financial support staff' (the people responsible for evaluating the risks entailed by a capital project and who negotiated with the banks) within the project teams. At first sight, this was unsurprising, as two opposing logics were at work here: a 'business' logic focused on developing the business and a 'financial' logic concerned with managing risks. Not only was this confrontation inherent to the launch and completion of projects, it could also be viewed as necessary and useful, as it allowed the firm to ensure that the project had properly factored in all of the parameters and that it was the outcome of a process of negotiation between two actors representing different interests. Indeed, this was a conflict that cropped up at all levels of the company, the senior managers being keenly aware of what could happen if they did not keep a tight grip on the financial risks.

But the closer we got to the local level, the more this opposition put the actors in an uncomfortable position, one that made them ill at ease, especially the financial staff. They expressed a true sense of frustration, and the company wanted to handle this situation as well as it could, otherwise it ran the daily risk of losing high-calibre, well-trained staff. For the time being, this 'naturally conflictual situation' was being handled by appropriately rotating the most exposed personnel. This allowed the company to remain proactive rather than submit to events, and to avoid feelings of guilt from becoming involved in over-conflictual relationships. This left one question: why was this otherwise perfectly natural clash of logics so acute and occasionally violent in this part of the world, causing concern throughout the company?

How does one lose hold of reality?

Let us first consider the symptoms that showed that the actors were 'progressively' losing their grip on reality. The 'support' staff, and particularly the financial staff, expressed their malaise bluntly. It had become a part of the daily life of the organization and was now a feature of it. The problem was that this malaise was growing increasingly radical, sometimes taking forms that suggested that the actors concerned had entered a vicious circle of confrontation that had robbed them of their sense of reality. In the following paragraphs, we take a closer look at this, from the most anecdotal to the most radical.

It all began in the featureless routine of managerial problems. The financial staff complained of a lack of 'recognition', which was pretty vague. But, as usual, this complaint, with its psychological connotations, was in fact a façade for a financial demand. These financial support staff worked hard – too hard, in fact, which was part of the problem – and they felt their pay did not match their efforts. Indeed, they were the only 'support' staff to stress this point. From this we may conclude that this 'complaint' about pay no doubt encompassed less visible dimensions of their situation. This was an initial expression of their discontent, whose causes they themselves were incapable of analysing.

Moreover, this was a population that 'rejected' its own organization. Not that these people criticized the company – indeed, they acknowledged its quality and high degree of technical expertise – but in the interviews the only part of their work they considered important was the part that brought them into contact with the outside world, namely the lending banks. While these financial advisers found the financial simulations they performed daily to be repetitious and uninteresting, negotiating the financial packages gave them a chance to display their skills and thus gain 'recognition'.

In addition, this population of advisers was unstable, with no desire to remain in this function. A first consequence of this instability was that they wanted to become developers, i.e., to hold the same job as the people with whom they were in daily conflict. They imagined that the developers enjoyed greater comfort and power than themselves. They claimed to have the necessary qualifications to become developers, citing the fact that some developers originally came from the finance function as proof of this. However, this instability had nothing to do with any lack of interest in the work. Some of its aspects were viewed as requiring a high degree of expertise and as crucial to the success of the company's projects. This was a result of over-working, which took on absurd proportions over time, with no one being able to halt the runaway train. This came as a shock when compared with the relative tranquillity of the other actors, particularly the developers, and this further embittered relations. Questions were asked, with a touch of nervousness on occasion, as to who did and who did not have the time to go to the cinema or take a weekend break.

Finally, these financial advisers took a detached, cynical view of their own way of working: they denounced their inability to stem the ever-rising sophistication of the mathematical models they used to assess and control risks. They employed a vulgar expression (readers can guess which) to describe themselves, in order to convey to what extent they were able to go into minute detail in order to evaluate the financial feasibility of a project. They were not joking; as if they treated it as an accepted norm in their activity. But these derogatory expressions reflected the fact that no one, and certainly not any of them, was able to take an unbiased look at the way the system works: the things these actors were doing were more and more absurd (it was they themselves who said so) and they were no longer able to estab-lish a connection between what they did and what was really needed, or with their consequences. Slowly but surely, they had tipped from a natural state of conflict that was healthy for the organization to a lose-lose situation over which the actors concerned no longer had any control.

Our analysis showed, first, that no one wanted this uncontrolled situation. Paranoia-inspired interpretations are of no help in under-standing how this machine ran out of control. What happened was the outcome of a series of events and decisions taken at all levels, which had come together now, amounting to a 'pile-up' nobody was able to manage. It all began with true 'pioneers', caught up in an exciting 'entrepreneurial' adventure. These trailblazers were of necessity all-rounders who were unstinting with their time and energy. They were recognized and rewarded for their success, but it was then that over-working came to be the norm, which in turn became the benchmark and the criterion for assessing newcom-ers. What had underlain the success of the 'founding fathers' had become a key yardstick, even though this organization was seeking to become more 'professional'. In this process, the 'historical' norm had become less and less legitimate and acceptable. Evidence of this state of affairs was the fact that the pace of work in the oldest units had returned to normal, whereas the new units continued to reproduce the old model of success through total commitment.

Why did this norm of over-activity affect the financial advisers in particular, who not only continued to apply it wherever they were but who were still frantically expanding it? The division asked its developers not to 'miss out' on business in a highly profitable but also highly competitive industry, yet, at the same time, the corporate level of the company had an instinctive horror of the slightest financial risk. Those 'on the ground' heard the first command, while the financial hierarchy heard the second. It is true that forecasting and managing risks demand ever more sophisticated models and calculations. However, no one tried to ascertain the limits to the exercise, to determine where to draw the line. As a result, the financial sphere was unwilling to let anything slip through its grasp (this was the logic of over-control) and, in order to do this, they constantly worked to develop their expertise to an ever-higher level, regardless of how much over-work this entailed for the members involved in its projects. And to make sure nothing was left to chance, the financial advisers added to the pressure of the basic task (calculation) ever more finicky controls that further aggravated relations.

This created an opening for dealing with a conflict everyone in the company knew about but no one talked about, namely that in the project development process, the developers were the free actors in the system. They had sole responsibility for the way they worked, giving them broad latitude. The financial advisers, on the other hand, were tightly constrained given the nature of their material. They were under significant pressure from their superiors to let nothing escape their scrutiny and were under equally significant pressure from the developers. The developers demanded speed and flexibility, the latter being a word calculated to irritate the people in finance. But the project managers were the interface with the client and needed to be able to view the project 'in the round'. To have as free a hand as possible, they tried to 'integrate' the different support people into their team. This put the finance staff at risk of becoming totally dependent on the developers, and they responded by making their calculations and models increasingly complex. In order to achieve this, they relied on the corporate level of the company and its obsession with minimizing risks. They 'tightened up' their demands and their controls, and in so doing carved out a degree of independence vis-à-vis the developers. As such, they were both victims and accomplices in the way in which the organization functioned. We can see why they were calling for this situation to be both recognized and 'recompensed'.

However, beyond disputing the facts, the system did appear to have run out of control, again through a failure to master the vagaries of its own procedures. Spiralling sophistication and endless lose-lose situations could have ended up breeding either an ominous form of paralysis or uncontrolled risk-taking. Developers were now starting to 'conceal' what they were doing from the financial advisers, withholding information, presenting them with *fait accomplis* and congratulating themselves. As such, there was little homogeneity within the teams, the common interest was shattered and everyone accepted this situation of 'every man for himself' as the presiding rule in a community that had ceased to exist. The numbers went on being crunched in a partial void, reinforcing fears of serious mistakes, to which the response was still greater sophistication. This is what happens in organizations that have destroyed simplicity and trust.

6
Trust Destroyed, Trust Rebuilt

We have seen how companies have an amazing capacity to destroy the trust that underpinned the early success of many of them. But the moment they start to replace the initiative, goodwill and thoroughness of their employees with processes and tighter controls, they send a clear message of mistrust, and that is how everyone understands it. Yet companies talk about this a lot, just as they like to talk about simplicity. In fact, they distrust it. Organizations – and not just companies – have a tendency to accentuate themes diametrically opposed to their practices. After all, in France political parties split in the name of unity and no one raises an eyebrow.

This is all the more surprising given that many companies state the idea of 'investing in people' as a priority. Attracting and retaining talent is central to any human resources policy. Giving people the means to exercise their skills in autonomous conditions, in an open environment and an atmosphere of mutual trust is the backbone of every recruitment officer's pitch and of a company's rhetoric when it looks at itself in the mirror to learn that it is the loveliest of them all. True, trust is a delicate subject, and I doubt whether companies have thought very hard about the mechanisms that underlie it. They treat it as a state of mind, and thus as an individual phenomenon, without seeking to understand its 'systemic' components. Their attitude is one of 'let's get on with it' and 'trust me', which merely breeds mistrust. So we need to help them to see more clearly and show them how trust can just as readily be shattered as built, depending on the mode of operation that is put in place.

Let's keep things simple to start with: knowing what everyone is supposed to be doing does not imply that each task needs to be analysed and dissected, and that how to perform it needs to be spelled out on paper. It would never occur to a family to write out a 'charter of family life' and pin it to the door of each room. Likewise, people don't put down in writing how to get up in the morning, eat breakfast, lunch and dinner, and how to get into bed at night. People know how to do all of this and understand what they need to do so that living together is not only possible but also pleasant. Does that mean, as is sometimes said – which is something of platitude – that it is the organization's growth that renders the formalization of each person's tasks in ever-greater detail unavoidable, thus engraving it in stone? As we shall see below, though, there is nothing inevitable about this.

What is trust?

What is lacking here is an understanding of what makes this trust, which is so eagerly sought and which ought to prevail in any organization, possible, whatever its size. If we do not trust others, it is because we do not know what they will do if a particular event occurs or if we tell them something important. As such, we regard them as 'uncertain' and their behaviour as unpredictable. Let's be clear: we cannot put this unpredictability down to erratic actors responding haphazardly to events. It is inherently 'strategic', since it robs us of the possibility of knowing what is important to others, and hence assessing our possible power over them. This is a simplified repetition of the phenomena of uncertainty so magnificently described by Michel Crozier in *The Bureaucratic Phenomenon*.[1] The more uncertain the actor, the greater his power and the less we can trust him.

Now let's reverse this proposition: what makes trust possible is the reduction of behavioural uncertainty, what philosophers – and this should be brought home to companies, which fondly use the term without always understanding what it means – call *ethics*.[2] Being 'ethical' in collective life does not mean being honest in the somewhat simplistic sense of the term: it means agreeing to make one's behaviour less uncertain. Indeed, this is the bedrock of a strong, lasting relationship.

But why should an actor agree to become more predictable, and in so doing giving up a little of his freedom in a sense, in favour of the community to which he belongs? It is the existence of 'rules of the game' that guarantee him that, if he 'comes out into the open', there will be limits to the way other actors can use that exposure. This is not a matter of setting down new rules and procedures on paper yet again, now that we have seen how devastating that can be. The aim here is for the actors concerned to define simply among themselves what is and is not acceptable in relations between them, and what sanctions to apply in cases of failure to abide by these rules of the game. This word 'sanction' may be misleading: we are not talking here about 'docking someone's pay' or issuing 'warnings', but rather of exclusion from a community that has created and accepted norms of its own.

I can recall the merger of two companies where the 'cultural audit' revealed profound differences in their practices. One of these concerned discipline with regard to decisions taken: in the first company, these were respected and so had force of law; in the second, to cut a long story short, they represented a good basis for discussion. This might raise a smile. In fact, this was a major obstacle to the smooth functioning of the new Executive Committee then being set up and to the possibility of establishing relations of trust among its members. Once everyone had staked out their territory, the first company saw this as an established fact and respected the decisions taken, while the latter saw it as a starting point to increase little by little its share of the cake, making it impossible to establish relations of trust between these players, who after all were just getting to know each other. The establishment of 'rules of the game' that were freely consented to might have ensured that what had been decided would be respected and that anyone seeking to expand his territory would thereby exclude himself from the Executive Committee. This is not a process, it is a rule of the game. It is not forced on anyone, given that it is freely consented to. The result is not mistrust but trust, which allows everyone to progress much further collectively. Here we will discuss two case studies of companies that have had to confront this question. The first killed trust by substituting a procedure-driven bureaucracy for it. The second, under the pressure of necessity, did the reverse, for the greater benefit of all, company and employees alike. To use a notion that I will expand upon in the final part of this book, it created a collective interest, something companies chase after in vain, because once again they do not clearly understand the mechanisms that make these communities possible and viable.

I will start with a look at one of the European subsidiaries of a cosmetics giant. This subsidiary was initially independent, before being acquired by the larger firm around ten years ago. It retained a high degree of independence until the parent company made another acquisition in a neighbouring country. The parent company then decided that the two ought to be integrated, and my work concerned this transition from autonomy to integration.[3]

To put it bluntly, this transition was not going well, prompting a wave of worry, anxiety and incomprehension, and consequently suffering and disengagement on the part of some of the actors. The outsider's first – admittedly naïve – reaction is to think what a pity this is. This is because here we had a traditional environment (that of the original company) that had now disappeared in practical terms, but which was omnipresent in people's minds, where the actors had found the work interesting, had been involved in it and invariably shown goodwill, in return for both financial and social recognition: to work for this firm was tantamount to a guarantee in the eyes of an employee's bank manager. The implicit contract between company and employees was clear and seen by both parties as a win-win situation. Even the takeover by the larger company (the Group) had been unable to overturn this equilibrium. The 'historical' managers of the acquired business had been kept on for a while, and they stood firm in opposing any attempt by the acquirer to get its hands on the new subsidiary. This is a film I've seen many times!

Equally traditional is the next chapter in the story: the acquisition of the second subsidiary by the Group led to a series of ricochets that radically altered the state of play. The first consequence was the departure of the original management team from the subsidiary that we were studying. This set the scene for an assertion of the intention to create an 'integrated group' by issuing standards, procedures and reporting systems (this is becoming something of a habit!) that were to be the same for all subsidiaries. For the subsidiary that concerns us, this came as all the more of a shock in that little or nothing was done to accompany the change. Although employees understood what was going on, this did not make the transition any easier. One of them described the changes he could see in his daily life:

'We're increasingly hemmed-in by rules. The regulatory aspect is constantly gaining strength with each passing day [a reference to the

European health authorities, which are continuously tightening up their surveillance of the cosmetics industry]. *It's the same thing for internal procedures. This is fairly recent. It's with the new acquisition. They told us now we're global ... OK, ... why not...'*

This evolution, which was experienced as a revolution, had given the impression that people were being taken in hand and were losing their autonomy, with procedures invading a world hitherto rooted in trust and simplicity. Actors naturally experienced anxiety and a sense of guilt at the difficulties they were having in adapting to this new situation, and in involving themselves and achieving the same quality as before. The reason was that these procedures had brutally added to the number and complexity of their tasks! As a result, the front-line executives – chemists, pharmacologists and skilled workers – desperately strove to protect their troops. They saw that this was in their interests: they realized that they had a lot to lose in terms of conscientiousness, commitment or loyalty from employees in these new management modes, which in fact tended to send a signal of mistrust. Others took refuge in fatalism, the last stage before discouragement:

> *'The longer this goes on, the more indicators, objectives and who knows what there are. We can't handle all of it at once. As a result, we never see things through. We move on to something else.'*

Alone, this excerpt ought to bring to the senior managers' attention the risks they faced: for the time being, the shock was a frontal one and the actors were mainly disoriented. But experience shows that, if nothing is done, the most dynamic employees will soon be 'playing' the new system. They will make use of the inevitable contradictions and duplication between these different indicators, procedures and so forth to carve out areas of autonomy from which it will be very tough to winkle them out. It's becoming something of a refrain to note that too much control kills control!

In addition to this initial picture was the fact that there were serious concerns over the future in the company, concerns intimately bound up with our age. What the subsidiary produced was not exactly in tune with the Group's new strategic direction, as it turned increasingly towards 'organic' cosmetics, abandoning its more traditional activities to the competition. The new management was making an effort to redirect its own production activities towards this, but employees seemed to be relatively unaware of this. On the contrary, they noted with growing concern the widening gap between what the subsidiary did and the direction in which the Group seemed to be taking it. Plants, in particular R&D centres, had been closed for no apparent reason in the employees' eyes, merely adding to the general sense of unease. In other words, this environment was becoming 'destructured'.

The transition from trust to distrust

Let us now try to take a closer look at how things worked in practice. In order to do this, we need to point out that the initial company, now legendary in the eyes both of those who knew it and those who had 'heard about it', used to enjoy an abundance of resources. This allowed the company to 'buy off' its employees, who indeed were very conscious of, and grateful for, the benefits they were receiving – often to their own great surprise! During the interviews, operators expressed amazement at the 'huge' unexpected bonuses they were sometimes given.

These actors still appreciated their material and human working conditions – and they constantly compared their situation with what they knew of outside circumstances – while noticing that these conditions were starting to deteriorate. They all said they were happy with their lot, while noting that their workmates were less and less so. This was an unmistakable sign of this population's latent concern:

> *'The supervisors take good care of me. They ask after me when I'm sick. The personnel management is good. We're far from being numbers ... but I don't think everyone agrees, by a long chalk. For example, people are starting to grumble about the working hours and the difficulty of the working conditions. It's the older ones who complain the most.'*

> *'The pay is good on the whole. I'm not complaining. The only thing is that people are starting to complain that our basic pay isn't much, and that good bonuses are fine, but they don't count towards our pensions.'*

Despite this, the provisional and dominant (but for how long?) model was that of relations of trust, reflected in a much-appreciated autonomy at all levels in the workplace, in return for which the employees displayed unfailing goodwill. This was the subsidiary's initial model, from the days when it was 'free', which gave its actors so much satisfaction and which still surprised new arrivals: the more they came from an environment that had already been standardized, the more they saw this as a lack of organization. All of the actors gladly depicted this trust in roughly the same terms:

> *'I'm very happy in my job, and I very much appreciate the way the assessment interviews are conducted. My superior trusts me and I have a lot of freedom in my work.'*

> *'Our bosses tell us what has to be done during our meetings, but then they're not on our backs all the time. They trust us.'*

Let's be clear who these 'bosses' were: employees were talking about their immediate supervisors. How could it be otherwise, given the distance between the different management echelons in this firm, where those not in direct contact with the 'grassroots' were perceived as far-removed, indeed distant? But that was how things had always been and this had never been a problem.

Even if this model of exchanging goodwill for autonomy was deteriorating under the pressure of procedures, the local actors were still trying to preserve its substance by adapting it to the altered circumstances: they were prepared to do what they could to make sure 'it works all the same' (appreciate the paradox here!), while their front-line managers tried to shield them from the flood of new procedures, which struck everyone as being of doubtful utility. What the actors, technicians and front-line managers had to say ought to have sounded the alert. Those who had 'undergone' these phases of rationalization described it in almost identical accounts:

> *'I know that the people behind me are doing all they can, as always. But it's getting harder and harder, because the procedures are stricter and stricter, with more and more controls. Sometimes we have to choose between quality and production, but you can't spend two hours working out how to tape a box so that it complies with the rules.'*

These invasive procedures were affecting all activities and sites. Few of our interviewees failed to refer to this spontaneously, apart from the new arrivals, as mentioned above. But for all of the others, the message they were getting was a message of mistrust, denials by senior managers and the Group notwithstanding.

This distrust was supplanting the earlier trust, although nothing was being read into this radical transformation. This is because companies love to give meaning to what they do. They even see this as an essential precondition of the employee buy-in, ever since the resounding flop of 'creating shareholder value'. In the case before us, what was given was non-meaning. This was something expressed by the employees, sometimes vehemently and sometimes with bitterness:

> *'Do you want an example of the sales reps' travel expenses? The rep enters them into his computer and sends them to me; I check them and validate them. I send them to accounts, which validates them again; then they go to another department, which does the same thing. Do you know the only added value of all that? It's that the sales reps don't get reimbursed on time.'*

> *'They give us a lot of responsibility, but we had greater freedom before. We have procedures that just slow us down, and we increasingly have the feeling we're being watched. They keep on asking questions that never used to get asked.'*

> *'My staff are fed up! Really fed up! Everyone's demanding reports, and frankly it's starting to be too much.'*

One can see the new model emerging, and this will come as no surprise to the reader: as often happens, this firm was entering a phase of procedure-driven integration, under pressure from its parent company, which had at last managed to 'take it in hand'. In so doing, it was undoing the traditional model, where the actors reached arrangements among themselves based on trust and guaranteed by universally acknowledged rules: 'I'll leave you alone, but the production gets done, whatever happens.' The managers not in direct contact with the employees, the 'corporate blokes' as they said with a hint of contempt, did not or did not feel themselves in a position to rein in the process. On the contrary, as the foregoing excerpts suggest, they were stepping on the accelerator, positioning themselves in what they perceived to be the increasingly dominant logic. And this strategy of accentuating the process was increasing the sense of bewilderment in the rest of the organization.

The protective role played by front-line management

The people trying to respond to this, as we have seen, were the front-line managers in all parts of the company. For them, their 'political' survival – in the honourable sense of 'governance of the city' – depended on it: they knew that if the traditional exchange deteriorated too much, sooner or later this would erode the goodwill of their staff. And the result would be the same in any firm: senior managers would hold them to account for this deterioration, failing to perceive (or, more likely, not wishing to perceive) the systemic dimension of the problem. What is more, they rightly foresaw that ultimately a plethora of rules and processes was bound to supplant their discretion, i.e., their free will, which gave them their power over their immediate subordinates.

The strategy of the front-line supervisors, then, was the exact opposite of what we observed in the non-front-line executives: they did not aggravate things, preferring to attenuate them, even if that meant putting them in desperate, sometimes even dangerous situations of over-work. They became the 'adjustment variable' of a system that had taken the bit between its teeth and now seemed unstoppable. Their subordinates had grasped this and were grateful to them:

> *'I can see our supervisors are under much more pressure than we are. They're always under stress. I wouldn't want to be in their shoes! On the other hand, I have to admit, it takes the heat off us.'*

> *'Am I working under pressure? Definitely not! It's OK. I'm fine. There's no pressure on me. But it's different for the boss. She's constantly running around to fill in the gaps.'*

Adopting a strategy of attenuation and compensation in an environment where actors are accustomed to doing their best is bound to prompt feelings of guilt and discouragement amongst them: being obliged to do more and more in order to keep the burden off other people's backs inevitably leads to the conclusion that sometimes this is simply not possible, however much energy one expends. Does this mean one isn't good enough? These people are putting pressure on themselves, via a mechanism of self-induced feelings of guilt, and they cannot keep it up, leading to a loss of self-esteem. We are but a short step from psychosocial hazards. The following quotes illustrate how the executives on the ground experienced this difficult situation:

> *'From time to time I have a lot of work, too much. That's probably because I've asked for it. I can't say no, and perhaps I don't know how to delegate. So I get overwhelmed, and it makes me feel anxious.'*

> *'What stresses me is that I like a job to be well done. I have difficulty leaving things half-finished. When I see customers' and distributors' complaints pile up, I feel terrible.'*

> *'There's ghastly pressure every day, which I try to avoid passing on. That comes from everything that there is to be done. Everyone wants data and makes urgent demands that are very hard to handle. If I wanted to do things right, I think things would be even worse. I spend my time dealing with emergencies.'*

> *'I'm working at 150 per cent. We have too much work. The demands keep coming in from all over the place, from our management and especially from the other departments. As part of the drive to improve our processes, they're always demanding more of us. Sometimes I've had enough, because I have the feeling I'll never cope. I have the general feeling of being overloaded, but I'd be hard put to say exactly what's wrong. I try not to shift all of this on to my staff, but they've got too much. They can't cope either.'*

This is a knock-on effect of the deluge of procedures and processes, which companies have difficulty seeing and hence dealing with. These shift the balance of the workload in different ways, adding to the burden on some to the point of becoming unbearable, while (more rarely) lightening the burden of others. With imbalances adding to imbalances, this leads to situations that suddenly 'blow up' without warning.

To sum up this case, it comes as no surprise to find that what was at work here was a pure 'system effect', which was being left untended for the time being. On the one hand, we had a parent company which, for reasons of its own, though no doubt closely connected with managerial fashion, decided to 'align' all of its subsidiaries; staff functions that accentuated the process, following a logic in which no one gave orders but everyone obeyed them; and a front-line management that bore the full brunt of this about-turn and strove to shield its subordinates from its consequences. The traditional commitment to one's work, based on a trust that had never been betrayed, suddenly found itself stymied by a rising tide of urgent demands, leading to discouragement, withdrawal, distress and suffering – take your pick. Trust had been shattered and it was hard to imagine it being replaced by processes, however harmonious they might be.

I will now turn to a situation that arose through very different circumstances from those discussed above. Not that there is nothing in common between the two, not that the managers were more clearsighted than those in the previous example, but the system had grown up in such a way that its decision makers had never had the latitude to institute niggling procedures and controls. Like Napoleon who, speaking of his soldiers, said 'I am their leader, therefore I follow them', they merely observed the situation and discovered that they were no worse off when all was said and done. For once, the constraints of human resources management discussed here acted as a cushion against the invasion of procedures.

The conservatism of contentment

This next case study concerned the distribution of mail in a large European country bordering the Mediterranean.[4] The first surprise was to find that, in a world where work has become a problem, a burden, a source of anxiety and suffering that can drive people to extremes, the postal workers here liked their work and were happy to do it, to the point where some thought of themselves as being privileged. But this contentment had its downside, for we know how hard it is to persuade people who are happy and contented in their work to change. Consequently, the workers took a dim view of the reorganization undertaken by their company to adjust to the reduction in the volume of mail, a phenomenon observed in all comparable countries. Indeed, I gave this study the following title: 'A contented population, which intends to stay that way.'

This 'conservatism of contentment' was reinforced by the comparisons these postal workers made with their family and friends, because most of them were familiar with other working environments. They came from a variety of backgrounds, arriving in the company either through family connections (a minority) or by chance, but never through an official job centre or labour exchange. This meant that these people were 'proactive'. Most had held other occupations, often far-removed from their present job, and were thus very able to take an informed view of their current situation. This merely bolstered their sense of experiencing something special and highly positive, in contrast to what life would be like if they worked in a factory, with its monotony and constant supervision. Indeed, the more the 'crisis' bred situations of stress and anxiety around them, the more these workers felt they lived in a 'cocoon', as they put it. Seen from this point of view, there were few differences among them, minor quibbles apart. But whether one was a city postal worker or a rural one, recent or long-standing, a civil servant or a contract worker[5] (the proportion was 50/50), job satisfaction was more or less the same. To be sure, the 'workload is increasing' and the redrawn post rounds[6] were 'causing problems for the clients', but this was all of minor importance in relation to the rest of the job.

Still more surprisingly, when asked to describe the positive or negative aspects of their work, none of these postal workers mentioned pay. A minority of workers even said they were satisfied with their pay. All this is consistent with the foregoing: in a world of 'McJobs', precarious jobs and internships, regular pay plus bonuses looked like a plum job. This omission to mention pay is a sociological 'marker', in the sense that not mentioning a topic in an open-ended interview is a sign that this topic is not a central concern for the interviewee. Plainly, this stemmed from the fact that the postal workers were in a position to top-up their pay themselves and in proportions of their choosing. The rule that allowed them to leave once the job was done gave them the time for a second job, even if that meant doing as much overtime as they wished inside the company. The decision lay with the postal worker, not his superiors, thus preserving his freedom. Thus, it is not surprising that the workers agreed to work for a relatively low wage when, to compensate for this, they enjoyed a great deal of freedom in their work, including in the choice of working hours, enabling them to compensate for this basic wage as needed. They had good reason to be contented!

Admittedly, there were nuances in the postal workers' assessments. To be sure, the increasing workload was a cause for concern, but only for the future, since this is not a problem right now. It was also true that there were 'pockets of discontent' arising from local situations: no doubt the older postal workers had greater reservations than the younger ones, with the former accusing the latter of being insufficiently committed to their work, which observation contradicts. But all this was part of the accepted rhetoric in organizations and did not detract from the general sense of satisfaction: it was good to be a postal worker in this firm, in this day and age.

An example of contentment in the workplace

Scratching beneath the surface, what made them so contented? The explanation was not to be found among the traditional grounds for satisfaction at work. As well as failing to mention their pay as either a positive or a negative factor, these postal workers made no mention of the job security they all enjoyed. And they were no different from the rest of the population in that respect, which was especially the case for the youngest amongst them: for them, precariousness was an inescapable part of the society they lived in, and even though their work contract gave them stability, they did not regard it as providing an inalienable guarantee of their job.

Therefore, we needed to look elsewhere for the reason for this highly positive 'subjective view' of the postal workers' situation. The answer lay in the job itself or, to separate out the task, the conditions in which the workers performed this work. These conditions formed a coherent, highly integrated whole and gave the postal worker the justifiable feeling that he controlled his life, pace of work and involvement in it. The reverse – and this is how they put it – would be 'conditioned' work (conditioned by the speed of an assembly line), fixed working hours, a foreman on their backs all the time and no room for manoeuvre. Taking a 'clinical' look at their behaviour when working, the first thing that stood out was their oft-repeated preference for 'getting outside' as quickly as possible. From this point of view, the mechanization of sorting, including in this sorting centre, had changed little in their behaviour. They still rose very early, earlier than necessary, and arrived at the centre at the time when they knew the van (the one bringing the mail) would arrive. However much final sorting they had before them, the time at which their round ended varied very little, which suggested considerable room for productivity gains. Above all, this meant that, for the postal workers, the time for the end of the delivery round was, and had to remain, a non-negotiable invariant. In other words, there was a 'scale of degrees of freedom' for this population that could be described in terms as simple as those spelled out by the actors themselves, namely: their presence in the sorting centre was the biggest restriction for them, so they wanted to cut the time they spent there to the absolute minimum required for the final sorting. The delivery round itself was an appreciable, and appreciated, moment of freedom and its end was the condition of their 'absolute freedom', the freedom to use their time as they wished. This is what might be called a 'structured' environment. A few interview excerpts illustrate how the postal workers managed their work:

> *'The negative bit in my work is the final sort. I have to be there at 6.30 am, but I get up at 5 and get there at 6. I get there early as it lets me get out sooner.'*

> *'What I like in this job is the freedom. As long as you do the work well and respect a few rules, you get a lot of freedom. Of course, there's the two hours you have to spend in the sorting centre. But as soon as you're out delivering, you're free, you're your own boss.'*

> *'In the mornings, we do an hour of sorting. There, it's true, there's a certain amount of pressure. You're not allowed to talk much, and you have to keep up, or the others will bawl you out. But once you're out, there's no one on your back, you do the round at your own pace. Once I'm outside, it's a pure pleasure.'*

There was no need for processes to make sure the work was done, and no need to measure time and motion – group pressure and the collective interest in getting the work done as quickly as possible saw to that. And there was no question of messing up either, because that would wreak havoc with the delivery round. This was because if the work in the sorting centre was carried out under pressure, the delivery round was more like self-employed work (my own pace, my clients, my know-how). So great was the contrast between these two phases that the postal worker sometimes had the impression that he had two working lives. The former was acceptable because it was the precondition for the latter, but there is little hesitation shown as to which he preferred. A comment is called for here: this self-employed worker logic made it difficult for management to extend the duration of the 'constrained time' relative to the period of 'semi-free time'. Furthermore, following this logic, the postal workers made the client – the recipient of the mail – their own in ways reminiscent of those described in Chapter 1.

This made the postal worker a 'marginal outsider', with one foot inside the organization and the other outside, with an undisputed monopoly over contact with the end customer. He derived a great deal of autonomy from this position, rooted in his (no doubt exaggerated) know-how. To entrench and expand this position, he offered his customer a kind of excess quality no 'normal' form of functioning could hope to match. This allowed him, at the appropriate time, to threaten his company with a serious decline in the quality of service offered to the client in the event of any change liable to undermine his advantageous position. This means that the postal workers applied the same strategy as France's professors of medicine in opposing hospital reforms: the latter mobilized their patients, the former their clients.

Individualism and personalized service

However, this personalization of service and excess quality, which had 'forged' the postal workers' image (doing the shopping, fetching cigarettes, medication or newspapers), also had its downside. These workers expressed a high degree of individualism (behaving like self-employed workers), which made it hard to introduce a collective dimension that could make the organization more flexible. The workers rejected the 'teamwork' dimension. This was seen as a threat, as undermining the attraction of the postal workers' work, what made it worth getting up early, accepting perfectly ordinary pay without discussion and suffering the rigours of winter while accomplishing exploits – all in the service of their clients, of course. Indeed, this is what allowed the postal workers to see themselves as the best bulwark against the arrival of competition, which they were now starting to see 'operating' in their territory. Consider these interview excerpts about the practice of 'excess quality':

> '*I know there are people where you shouldn't ring the bell in the morning because they're asleep. So either I go back at the end of my round, or I know I can leave a recorded delivery letter with a neighbour. It's the same for periodicals. Older people like them to be delivered at a precise time. I try to respect that.*'

'You know, people give us a very warm welcome. They invite us in for a coffee, and we run all sorts of small errands for them: stamps, medication, cigarettes, etc.'

'With clients, we're part of the family. Some people see us as the Messiah. So we perform little services, changing the gas bottle or light bulbs. We bring them bread and medications.'

'There's no letterbox to post mail in the vicinity of the big stadium where I do my delivery round. So I get out of my van, I leave the window open, and when I get back it's full of letters.'

This handful of quotations inspires one amusing comment. The postal workers spoke without restraint of 'customers'. Unions in some European countries instinctively recoil at the thought of doing so and prefer the term 'user'. This is no mere nuance. The user is someone who 'uses', to whom something is made available, in a relationship that does not imply that the customer dominates the person delivering the service. On the contrary, this user 'needs' the service, and the balance of the dominant-dominated relationship is tipped in favour of the person providing the service, in this case the postal worker. To agree to shift from this to the notion of 'customer' is to reverse the dependency and recognize that one is 'in the service of ...', with all that that may entail for working conditions. The postal workers had made this transition without quibbling, because they knew it was in their interests: they had moved on to serving the public, while their unions were still talking about public service.

What is more, their working conditions were not a problem for them. On the contrary, this youthful population, with a rapidly growing proportion of women, felt very good about its very special working hours (starting very early and ending very early). This was because these hours gave them a chance to care for their children in the afternoon or to top-up their pay as much as they wished.

This was a highly individualistic world. There was little mutual help, with each person learning mainly on his own, and the small proportion of collective work they had to do (the final sort) was not conducive to solidarity. The company had sought with mixed results to develop collective working, but without creating any sense of solidarity. Following a well-known pattern, some interviewees reported that there was solidarity within their team, but none outside.

Clearly, solidarity is a positive word in the ambient culture, so one must say one participates in it. But in reality no one did, and they expressed that by ascribing this 'defect' to the others. But once 'socialization' was completed, they all accepted and assumed their extreme individualism:

> 'No, we don't talk much. It's a world of individuals. No one asks if we need help. It never occurs to the older ones to help the younger ones.'

> 'Individualism rules here. If we helped each other more, perhaps we'd get on a bit better. Some rounds are longer than others, but they never offer to lend a hand.'

A final tangible dimension of this contentment with their work was the lack of ambition in this population, with no desire to apply for possible promotion. The company was constantly opening up opportunities for them, but young and old alike were reluctant to apply. Why should they? They had achieved a highly satisfactory balance between working hours, pay and freedom. Their priority was stability and preserving the status quo, even though they could have improved their circumstances. This is a fine illustration of the contrast between satisfaction with one's work and acceptance of change. Here is how the workers accounted for this form of 'collective passiveness':

> 'I have no plans to get ahead, take on responsibilities, add to the stress. I'm not sufficiently motivated by money.'

> 'Do I want to get ahead? It's not on my agenda. I want to start by getting settled and buy myself a delivery round.[7] After that, it will almost certainly be no. I want a quiet life above all.'

> 'No, I didn't want promotion. In addition, I might have been required to go somewhere else. And in any case, I've seen the pressure they [the bosses] are under.'

These are excerpts from interviews with postal workers of all ages working in very different parts of the country. The interviews revealed what the reader has surely begun to realize by now, namely that, for the moment at least, this was not a stressful job. As we shall see below, none of the workers had the impression of being under pressure and, to be frank, the very notion raised a smile.

Above all, though, in their 'counter-model', what really extinguished all ambition was the 'bosses', the people they observed daily. The 'boss' was anyone who not only performed the postal worker's work but who also took on special responsibilities. There were the team leaders, of course, in the most conventional sense of the term, but the company had also introduced 'quality postal workers', who spent part of their time on more administrative tasks in the sorting centre, such as verifying rounds, handling customer complaints, etc. Nobody envied them, as we have already seen. This was because, in reality they had served as the 'adjustment variable', absorbing the additional workload created by each of the reforms implemented by the company. They had taken responsibility for organizing the delivery rounds, dealing with any resulting hitches, in other words anything liable to upset the smooth running of the postal workers' lives. So, for these workers, it was a question of the more things change, the more they remain the same. From this we may conclude that, if genuine changes were to affect the present balance, the postal workers would adjust the speed of mail delivery to preserve their most precious asset: the time at which they ended their round.

It is interesting to observe how such a structured world reacted to the changes its organization was seeking to implement. These, it should be borne in mind, were intended to increase flexibility by making it possible for postal workers to take on all or part of another delivery round. Attempts to date had yielded mixed results. Flexibility had been 'outsourced' to others, the 'quality postal workers' especially. This had gone smoothly since, as in any organization where one of the actors 'controls' access to the customer, the postal worker's power placed his superiors in a position of dependency. At the same time, though, these actors were sufficiently 'intelligent' to refrain from pressing their advantage too far, so as not to upset the existing, highly satisfactory balance. Instances of deterioration in the climate between postal workers and their superiors were rare and highly localized, and the company handled them skilfully.

All this explains why the postal workers' response to the company's plans swung between indifference – they won't change much – and worry – yes, they could change things. Their fears, when they expressed them, centred on an increase in their workload. But this was a 'soft' fear: the postal workers could clearly see the decline in the overall volume of mail. They knew that 'advertising mail' was replacing conventional mail as the new 'growth driver', or at least was acting as a means of slowing the decline. Consequently, they paid lip service to the notion that adding a few streets to their round was being offset by the overall fall in the volume of mail handled. And, as we have seen, whenever there was an additional workload to be handled, it was the 'quality postal workers' or even the team leaders who did the work. All of the actors implicitly agreed that, for a given workload, the quality postal workers would sometimes stay at the sorting centre to 'produce quality', still a vague notion in the postal workers' eyes. But as soon as an incident occurred, shift postal workers (another of the company's inventions) and quality postal workers 'got out (on strike)', sometimes for extended periods. This was the reason why the postal workers did not seek promotion, especially to this kind of responsibility. It was a wry paradox to find bosses who could not see what was so special in what they were doing, while the others had no desire to take over their job because they seemed to be under constant pressure. Let's listen again to what the postal workers had to say:

> 'The quality postman is constantly out doing the rounds! He ought to stay in the office to update the lists. Well, it's me that does mine.'

> 'The quality postmen do replacements and help out. I think they're called that to give them a name. Otherwise, I don't see what's so special about what they do.'

> 'The quality postmen and the shift postmen, I haven't a clue what they do. Perhaps they look to see whether the delivery round logbooks are up to date. But one thing I'm sure of is that they do replacements.'

Mobilizing the customer against the organization

It is a fair bet that there are 'strategic' reasons for this ignorance, which explains why protest against changes was mainly preventive in intent. Not surprisingly, it claims to speak in the name of the customer and the service provided. The customer was the postal worker's shield; the pace of work was his freedom, and he rationalized this first and foremost as guaranteeing the quality of service provided to the customer. By definition, any attempt to reassert control over this pace of work was bound to impair the quality of this service. We are back where we started.

This explains the protests against the plan to introduce a degree of modularity into the rounds. This plan constituted a breach in the postal worker's monopoly over the customer, even if it would help to teach the customer that he cannot expect to have the same postal worker indefinitely. This 'learning process' is not unimportant, for it is hard to mobilize the customer over the reduction of a cost he does not pay – or at least not directly – when he receives mail paid for by the sender.

Yet it is these customers that the postal worker mobilized in order to contain this trend towards an increasingly collective, continuously less autonomous pattern of work that consequently undermined the existing balance. It is a good lesson in terms of change strategy. This is a far cry from brutal measures to seize control by means of processes and reporting. This company was changing very progressively, with no direct impact on what was still non-negotiable for the postal workers. But the postal workers understood that they could not hold on to their advantages indefinitely, and that they would have to give ground on this in order to preserve this situation. They seemed ready for this negotiation, given the way they were already exaggerating the impact of the first reforms:

> *'We serve the public, after all! And people need to be able to come and see us at the same times. What's happening is totally ridiculous. A customer might see four different postmen in a week. It's idiotic.'*

> *'They bungled the introduction of the changes. My colleagues had great difficulty learning new streets. I can tell you we've gone backwards in terms of quality of service. The customers make no secret of what they think.'*

> *'These modular rounds are hell. Customers can't understand, even though we explain it to them.'*

This left the question of the 'new services', those additional tasks that the company was planning to ask its postal workers to perform in order to compensate for the steady decline in the volume of mail. Not surprisingly, this prospect aroused considerable misgivings, which were a logical outcome of all of the above issues. The concept of service had a very special meaning for the postal workers: it meant 'performing a service', i.e., a voluntary act of free will that was unremunerated (at least officially). This vision of service put the postal worker in a 'dominant' position and assisted in capturing the client. From this perspective, service merely accentuated the intrinsic characteristics of the 'postal workers' system'. Anything that came to hand would do in challenging this trend towards *selling* services decided by the company to the customer: this would reverse the situation of dependency between customer and postal worker, with the former paying directly for the aforementioned services.

The stakes were not small and threatened to disrupt the postal worker-customer-company triangle. Diversifying services and introducing payment for them reintroduced the postal worker into the company and de facto modified his traditional relationship with the customer. He was therefore bound to be highly critical of this initiative, even if he grudgingly understood its logic and the need for it. His criticism came as no surprise: they're snatching work away from professionals, which is immoral in a period of high unemployment; we're not qualified to perform these potentially complex tasks; it isn't provided for in the work contract. One postal worker put it this way:

> *'I'm not interested in selling new services. There are people who are qualified for that, and in addition it's what brings home the bacon for them. What's more, they'd need to train me. No, it isn't a good idea.'*

What clearly emerged in this company is that regulation and striking a balance between the different actors' strategies had taken the place of management by constraint, rules and procedures. One might point out, with a wry smile, that there was no less 'integration' here than elsewhere: the actors had no need of embarrassing processes in order to adopt the same practices. These were not 'dictated', they were 'generated' by the context. The actual degree of control exercised by management hardly mattered at this point. It could not be less than what we might find in 'fragmented' firms, where the plethora of norms of all kinds leaves everyone free to act as they please. Quite simply, to use the good old rhetoric of management, we may consider that this organization was not under control, that 'officially' people did what they liked, and so on. And this was effectively a risky system for the managers, as it deprived them of the possibility of hiding behind failure by their highly undisciplined personnel's failure to respect the standards laid down, should the need arise.

The Americans have a very apt, though slightly vulgar, expression to describe these ubiquitous protection strategies.[8]

There was scope for genuine change here, thanks to this spontaneous 'integration'. Instead of arguing that the need for this change was a question of common sense, and that one would therefore have to be dishonest or sick to reject it, management was well aware of its scope for negotiation and where the lines were that must not be crossed. It knew what the dominant actors would not sacrifice under any circumstances, and this knowledge broadened its scope for negotiation. In a word, this organization had displayed great maturity, even if it did not fit into the conventional fundamental rules of management. This is not a matter of concern for the organization, but it is for the fundamental rules of management.

Part III
Can We Do Things Differently?

7
The Difficulty of Changing Endogenous Organizations

When one lets work or the customer slip, one creates near-insurmountable handicaps that are tackled only when driven by necessity. This explains why, unsurprisingly, change is always more reactive than proactive. But generally it remains purely 'cosmetic'. To be properly thought out, well-designed and genuine, change requires a thorough understanding of how things work in reality, rather like what I have tried to share with the reader in the case studies in this book. That is what distinguishes structure, where modifications brought about through succeeding 'reorganizations' change little, from how an organization actually functions and, in the process, enables us to identify the levers available in order to change the way actors behave. This is because this is the key, as we have seen in some of the examples in previous chapters: as long as we do not change what people do, we have done little but paper over the cracks, hence the expression 'cosmetic change'.

This satisfies many people. It guarantees them that something has been done while minimizing the risk to the person who did it. It is an awkward exercise that calls for time, tenacity and imagination. And the example comes from the top: how many plans, projects and missions have set about 'reforming government', yet culminated, breathtakingly, with government continuing to turn out a mediocre product at great expense? This explains, once again, the frantic recourse to processes, informants and reporting techniques which, as we have seen already, create more confusion than clarity or positive outcomes.

The persistence of this error reveals the degree of confusion in the face of the scale of the task. So great is the confusion that top managers turn to other fields, such as strategy and finance, leaving the heavy responsibility of adapting the organization accordingly to their 'intermediate bureaucracies'. These bureaucracies throw themselves into the task, as we have seen, coming up with inoperative solutions through their causal reasoning and over-regulation. As such, companies today are faced with a genuine problem of reasoning, and we are unlikely to find a way out anytime soon. All the prescriptions and modelling now invading management disciplines – one can hardly call them sciences – represent a step backwards in comparison with the progress made in the post-war era regarding our understanding of the mechanisms of collective action.[1] The days when people sought to understand the problem before looking for the solution are over. The solution is now to be found in the drawers of consulting firms, who make it all the more complex to justify the army of consultants (preferably young – who are paid less – to keep the firm's 'margins' up) needed to 'deploy' it.

The implicit alliance between these consultancies and the intermediate bureaucracies works like a charm. The former have the solutions to lend legitimacy to what is to be done, providing the latter with 'grist to the mill' to ensure their survival and, if they play they cards right, their power. Going a step further, here we consider the main reason why the social sciences have never turned into a management discipline, leaving aside a handful of 'niches', except where practised as a minor art form by the occasional enlightened CEO. To find their place in the dominant management ideology, they would have to agree to being 'bastardized' and to jettison insight in favour of prescription. That is when one begins to hear such peremptory, meaningless utterances as 'there's no problem without a solution' or 'a problem without a solution is not a problem'. This is a dismal situation. Consequently, I want to try to demonstrate, through two more case studies, the extreme complexity of trying to effect change in endogenous organizations, a process that cannot be boiled down to a handful of ready-made prescriptions or mechanistic commands.

The first case study took place in a broadcasting company that wanted, for considerations of cost, to merge two job categories that previously handled support and production for broadcasts, namely technicians and production assistants, into a single category, 'production technicians'.[2] At first sight, there were few surprises in this organization. As in most of the work environments we have seen so far, the actors strived to protect the area of autonomy and comfort they had carved out for themselves during the life of this company, while the company itself had never been all that particular about this until now. As one of the technicians, who represented the key population in this environment, said:

> *'Lots of technicians are like me: they don't want to be in direct contact with journalists. They want to keep their independence.'*

The logic of 'do as you like'

At the same time, all of the actors expected the planned changes to undermine 'acquired rights', hitherto guaranteed by a relentless social control that kept everyone in line. For the time being, however, this was a highly stable organization that revolved around the journalists/ technicians nexus, functioning according to a classic attraction/ repulsion pattern. But this was also a highly 'administrative' organization, whose endogenous character largely took precedence over the needs of the environment, the audience or the shareholders. This was especially visible in the pre-eminence of the logic of 'do as you like' in all of the actors' choices, which took precedence over considerations of necessity or cost. As one executive said on the subject of the technicians:

> *'Nowadays, their work has nothing to do with the company's needs, but with what they fancy doing, their family demands or others.'*

Similarly, there were norms which, seen from the outside, might suggest some laxity but which in fact reflected the daily realities of an environment where necessity, represented by a distant, invisible payer, had no place. The idea that it might be necessary to 'do more with less', and that the organization of the work might be the variable by which to achieve this, was therefore unthinkable. Finally, we found that management had taken a back seat, judging from the difficulty interviewees – technicians especially – had spelling out clearly who their boss was. And when we did identify them, these bosses themselves appeared to spend their time and energy on marginal or symbolic activities. One told us:

> 'We've decided to take back a certain number of things in hand to restore some discipline. For example, I'm going round the offices to get people to stop smoking. It's important to show that the rules have to be respected.'

A technician had this to say in reply:

> 'My technical superiors ... yes ... there's lots of them. In fact, it's exhausting the number of offices you have to check with to get the information you need. In fact, to find out who's in charge, it depends on the problem, that's it...'

As such, the system worked autonomously, with no regard to hierarchy, and was capable of selecting the 'good people' unaided: these were the ones who got called first, even if that meant leaving the less capable ones undisturbed. It was therefore 'regulated', but unlike the case discussed in the previous chapter, regulation here had a high cost, with no guarantee of quality for the client (the listeners). But asking about the cost of a cultural product prompts a furious response, as is well known.

Having said that, it was striking to note that the denial of economic reality worked both ways: to be sure, no one wanted anybody to measure what this organization produced, yet at the same time, none of the interviewees cited pay as a positive or negative aspect of their work. This reinforced the pressure for immobility across the organization, around an implicit bargain that was clear to all: that no one must upset the system's fragile equilibrium and that the actors would handle the financial side of things themselves.

Another 'classic' feature of endogenous organizations is that all of the actors realize the need to change their way of working. Executives, trade unions and all employee categories agree, one way or another, on the need to adapt. This is a crucial observation: it shows that the difficulty of bringing about change in this kind of organization stems less from the content of decisions taken than from how they are taken, explained and implemented. The main point, then, is the method rather than the content. This means that solutions that spring fully-formed from managerial common sense, or are imposed in its name, will have no chance of success. One has merely to recall the upheavals at Air France in the early 1990s, until a new chief executive required all categories of personnel to work out possible solutions of their own, step-by-step, some of which were then approved by referendum.

In this instance, many factors were inciting personnel to take a clear-eyed view of things, including the arrival of new technologies simplifying their work and the example offered by the competition, of which many of these actors had first-hand experience given the ease of moving between channels. There were also many other factors besides this one. But, as usual, an understanding of the unavoidability of change was not sufficient to ensure its acceptance without fear or discussion. The older technicians and journalists saw in these changes a slow yet inexorable decline in what made their jobs so special. They had no wish to be confronted with a *fait accompli*, still smarting from certain earlier reforms that left a weighty legacy of mutual distrust. This was something expressed by a technician in the following quote:

> *'People are seriously demotivated at this channel. The transition to an "all news" formula left deep scars, especially among the technicians who have been here a long time. They found they'd become button-pressers, and it's a bit like that for the producers, who used to have a bigger role. In fact, nothing's been done to encourage people to do a good job.'*

His views were echoed by this journalist:

> *'We journalists were never consulted about the reforms to the technical side. We're expected to adapt.'*

Added to this was the absence of a front-line management (clearly, it is a constant in this type of organization that this echelon gets sacrificed), which meant that senior managers had no day-to-day contact with what was going on. To complete this initial description, we were dealing here with a highly individualistic environment, scattered among a number of micro-categories that then ran themselves, making it hard to identify a common interest. Let's try to gain some deeper insight into how this worked.

As we saw earlier, it is the way people in the cultural sphere perceive the nature of work that leads them to shun the logic of necessity in favour of that of 'do as you like' and to define their own personal work norm accordingly. Preference is thus naturally given to endogenous needs (those of the individuals) to the detriment of exogenous ones (those of the radio station and, in the final analysis, those of its listeners). A technician described the situation very well:

'We choose our work rosters much more on the basis of the working hours that suit us than on what we are capable of doing.'

Thus, it was not easy to 'keep things going': it was necessary to 'propose' and rely on volunteers, while taking a very permissive line on people's working practices, the pace of work and their degree of commitment.

As one executive noted:

'I see people, I propose broadcasts to them, I put them in touch with journalists. But it's hard, because the people in this organization are used to being cool. A woman production assistant told me: "you know perfectly well I don't work on Monday!" Some even moonlight; everyone knows about it.'

Another technician added candidly:

'I've nothing against the idea of expanding the system of production technicians if there are volunteers for that.'

One category, two strategies

Individuals were allowed a great deal of freedom in this environment, giving the observer the impression that he was dealing with a 'federation of self-employed workers'. The technicians had devised two strategies that allowed us to understand the ambiguity of their position relative to the 'production technicians' plan. Some of them adopted a perfectly classical strategy of withdrawal: they 'did their job', but never committed to the relationship with those with whom they were supposed to work as a result of the reorganization, the journalists in particular. These people had no wish to be part of a team (as in producing a regular magazine, for instance) and asked to be assigned to a studio (where different programmes were made), provided there was a rotation of journalists and producers in that studio.

This approach focused on the purely technical aspect of the occupation, to the exclusion of any other form of collective involvement that could turn one into the journalist's 'helper'. That was the risk they perceived with the transition to 'production technician'. The issue of being assigned to a journalist altered the relationship with him, and this was something this group of technicians rejected. They did not want to be pinned down and wanted to continue 'roving' between different programmes. This category was aiming for a 'double whammy': preserving their occupation, while maintaining a highly advantageous state of autonomy and choice in the process. Again, necessity and economic constraint had no place in this line of reasoning. Added to this was the not inconsiderable fear of having to acquire new skills, which is all the harder when one is wrapped up in one's 'defensive routine'.[3] This was something expressed by a technician:

'Maybe I wouldn't mind becoming a production technician. But I don't necessarily have the skills to be a producer. For example, researching music for the magazines demands a certain amount of background culture, which I don't have. I don't know how to acquire it.'

To make the point about the complexity of this type of organization and hence the difficulty of getting it to change, it is worth noting that the rejection of the idea of being dependent on the journalists did not preclude short-term alliances with them (reflecting the attraction/repulsion relationship). This alliance hinged on the preservation of professions and employment statutes: for the journalists, and especially those going out – or hoping to go out – to make documentaries, the issue of being accompanied by a technician was a kind of 'visible sign of wealth'. It avoided the risk of 'degrading their profession', as would be the case if they themselves had to perform the technical aspects of their broadcast or documentary. With that in mind, preserving the technician's profession as such was the essential condition for preserving the journalist's profession as such. In practice, the 'first viewer' theory applied here, whereby it was deemed to be very useful to have someone accompanying the production who could pass an initial judgment on the journalistic quality of what had just been, or was about to be, broadcast. One journalist very clearly spelt out the link he saw between the survival of the two professions:

> '*As a journalist, of course, I can do it all myself. But in that case, I may make a complete hash of things, or do everything less well. I would miss having the other person's opinion. No ... all that is a question of economics alone. One increases the range of the people one hires, and they become jacks-of-all-trades. Technicians are being asked to do more, and that economic logic makes for poor television.*'

As we can see, the journalist was not asking for a technician to accompany him all the time, he simply wanted to preserve a function that would guarantee the integrity of his own profession.

The second strategy employed by technicians, and apparently the one favoured by the younger technicians, was to accept this 'face-to-face' with the journalist in exchange for a broadening of his role. Here, teamwork took priority, especially in the production of magazines. In so doing, the technicians were taking out insurance on their future, having glimpsed how things could evolve. But there was no question for them of accepting things blindly. They stated four conditions in our interviews: being given the necessary training; being paid in a manner commensurate with the fact that they performed 'two occupations in one'; maintaining acceptable working hours; and clearing up the situation of those on 'precarious' contracts. The latter had until now met the organization's need for flexibility, but they faced an uncertain future as a result of drastic cuts in the radio station's budget.

Indeterminacy spells freedom

Continuing our examination of this company, let's now take a look at the production assistants. The production assistants probably formed the most mixed population in the radio station. A variety of paths led to this occupation, though people largely arrived as a result of chance encounters. Unlike the technicians, they did not form a cohesive group and they had no professional identity. For them, their identity lay in the quality of their contribution to a broadcast, especially when the accompanying music played an important part. Their main strategy, therefore, was to seek out interesting 'niches', including production in general and magazines in particular. Once they had found that, they placed themselves 'under the protection' of a producer or journalist with whom they formed a symbiotic working relationship. This was the reverse of what most of the technicians did. At the same time, this strategy afforded them considerable comfort in their work, giving them a great deal of freedom to avoid the pressures of live broadcasts or the monotony of routine. One production assistant expressed the following views:

> 'The magazines are mainly produced by stable teams. We are assigned to two or three programmes, always with the same people. We can work better with the journalists. The best thing, of course, is the weekly magazines. We have three programmes to produce in the week, and we're free to organize with the other people as we like. Compared to that, working on news is much more mechanical.'

> 'The working period doesn't stop when we leave. We work again in the evenings, for example, to look for music. News is more like working on an assembly line. We don't have to think outside of it.'

It was hard to keep track of the amount of work necessary and the amount actually done in this kind of work. This indeterminacy, by definition, bred freedom. The limits to this strategy of autonomy lay in the station's move towards an 'all-news' format (especially in sport), which thus cut down on the type of programme preferred by the production assistants. In a sense, the noblest part of the profession was on the way out, in favour of conflating the professions of producer and technician into a single role. The realism of these producers, and especially their lack of choice, forced them to sign up to the change, anticipate it and prepare for it. Failing that, this population could well have found itself in an impasse. Moreover, adopting the production technician system would not only help to protect for the future but would also give them a better handle on their present work. They no longer depended on the technicians to achieve the level of quality they believed to be their hallmark. As such, shifting to this method of working implied regaining some of their autonomy, including in the news programmes, which is where they would have to go at some future point in time. Here is how one producer described the situation:

> *'Sometimes, when we produce a really well-made programme, we come across technicians who are true craftsmen … but sometimes, too, they have no special skills, they are not motivated, and that's a problem for me. That's why I tend to be in favour of the production technicians system, because people here are so unmotivated.'*

For this category, the quality of the work done was imperative if the producers were to stand out. Thus, they were willing to play along – their future work partly depended on it – provided the project was more than just a simple economic project and was inspired by a desire to create a high-quality radio broadcast. Fair enough, but this category was 'weak', because it was poorly organized. For management, therefore, it did not provide much in the way of support.

However, it is worth noting here the extreme variety of strategies employed by the different actors, making this a highly variegated system. Yet the 'habit of freedom', which colours the different categories' perceptions and actions, would surely lead them to see the issue of change in terms of potential allies, levers and bargaining over what was acceptable and what was not – far more so than in terms of orders from above, new norms or imported 'best practices' that may have proved successful elsewhere. I will return to this in my conclusions on this case.

Forging ahead on what had come to resemble an expedition without an end, it is worth noting that the lack of front-line management, as already pointed out, had fostered the logic of 'do as you like' and the quest for ever more protective areas of autonomy. During the interviews, the very idea of management struck interviewees as bizarre. Thus, the personnel department had taken the place of this deficient or non-existent local management. There was some logic in this, since every workplace conflict in this company turned out to be a problem of labour relations. One production technician (so some did accept the change!) described his understanding of the system:

> *'Here, the atmosphere at work is very cool. In the station I used to work at, there was a real hierarchy, with real bosses. Here, I've got loads of*

bosses, which means I don't have any. Only the journalists have a real comic opera army of them. As long as there are no problems, everything's fine. If not, I go straight to Personnel. When I became a production technician, I went to see Personnel. I've never needed to see my bosses.'

The main result of this was that the personnel department in question was overwhelmed with work, requests and decisions to be taken – the kind of vicious circle sociologists love! Needless to say, this logjam ruled out any kind of sanction, whether positive or negative, for the system neither punished nor rewarded. Everything was based on negotiation and the goodwill of the actors concerned. In this company, everyone did as he pleased, for good or ill – more for good than for ill, in fact – and everyone said 'I' and never 'we', since nobody stood for the general interest. It is worth noting in passing that some companies actually ban people from starting a presentation with 'I' (cf. the US oil and gas giant Chevron).

Pulling further on this thread, unsurprisingly we found that this system gives great importance, de facto, to the trade unions, the only people the personnel department dealt with, occupying some of the void left by the absence of management. Unions and personnel steered the system as well as they could, while individuals organized themselves according to their tastes and needs. But here we found – and this is where our journey ends – that this self-organization around the logic of 'do as you like', which initially came as such a surprise to the outside observer, was a *consequence* of the prevailing anomie. This had now produced a stable, conservative system that also caused anxiety among the actors, who were not especially happy in it. As ever, the cost of this mode of operation was externalized to the shareholder, who was hitherto not especially curious or demanding. But things were changing, and this environment would be forced to move as well.

This book is not a textbook of change management. Nevertheless, the complexity of this analysis and its systemic dimension suggest a somewhat frustrating game of billiards. It raises the question as to how to escape from it other than via a major crisis, the customary way in which endogenous organizations re-enter the real world. I shall try to answer this question in the next chapter. But here, briefly, are a few pointers. There are no easy solutions here: no model ready to be imported either; no 'process for the production and broadcasting of a programme'(!), with defined functions, set working hours, reporting modes and indicators of good management. On the contrary, it is necessary to pinpoint the populations capable of playing a part and the factors enabling progress without impinging (initially at least) on what is non-negotiable for them; gaining insight into the true problems (anomie, lack of front-line management), in contrast to all those things that appear 'shocking', e.g., under-working or the logic of 'do as you like', and which 'tough' management is supposed to remedy. In other words, change with people, not against them.

*

Endogenous organizations are especially able to resist the changes their management (sometimes) want to impose on them when they succeed in mobilizing the customer in their cause. That is understandable, insofar as we have already noted that only pressure from the outside environment, or a change in it, can jolt the organization into movement. In the market sector, it is the advent of competition that plays this role, by curtailing the opportunities for externalization. This is why it is not uncommon to see some of the most modern companies, including ones embodying the 'new economy', relentlessly striving to restore their monopolistic situation while under constant threat from new arrivals. That is what Microsoft has been doing with great perseverance, and not surprisingly the level of satisfaction among this company's customers is well below that of users of French government departments, which is saying something! It also helps us to understand that the quarrel over the comparative efficiency of the public and private sectors is to some extent a false debate. The difference is between competition and monopoly, between the capacity to externalize and the need to cut costs and improve quality. But a captive customer, or one who is convinced that this organization serves him best, whatever the competition, can be mobilized on behalf of the members of this organization: who could imagine that all one has to do is to throw the skies open to all airlines for travellers to think they are all equally safe?

The situation is all the more blatant in healthcare, where the ability to mobilize the patient one has treated, is about to treat or whom one may one day treat is a fearsome weapon in the hands of people working in the sector. This explains why it is so hard to introduce change in hospitals. I had the good fortune to assist one of these processes in a major European capital. Without question, the patients in this country were well cared for, with a rate of noso-comial (hospital-acquired) infections close to zero, one of the lowest in Western Europe.

When the collective interest suffers a lack of legitimacy

As everywhere in Europe, the managers of this hospital cluster, which we will call the 'Institution', wanted to 'rationalize' it by combining units and hospitals based on a 'medical plan' framed by a brand new Department of Strategy.[4] As we shall see, the hurdles to be overcome were considerable: the fragmented nature of the medical world was one of these, suggesting 'piecemeal' reactions and hostilities complicating the task of forging a common front among those opposed to change. But the reverse was the case in reality, in the sense that any decision taken in the collective interest, for example, that of the Institution, had no legitimacy other than in the eyes of people working at the level of the Institution. The Institution was having trouble asserting its 'brand' in the face of local, sometimes very local, brands. Probably the hardest transition to manage was to encourage doctors to abandon the logic of the independent professional (even if they worked in a hospital) in favour of that of a collective mode of operation.

Similarly, all the sources of comfort in the working lives of all these people, which some accepted and others challenged, but which were real enough, left little room for manoeuvre. Among doctors and other occupational categories alike, these sources of comfort were reinforcing their anxiety regarding a future where things could only become tougher, as far as they could see. This had prompted radical hostility on the part of the most extreme elements of the workforce, those who had decided to come out fighting – presumably because they believed they had important things to fight for – and passivity and withdrawal on the part of those who knew they had no choice but to knuckle under, whatever happened.

Faced with this situation, it would be tempting to force change through by taking strong action, showing that there would be no way back, radically changing the dominant logic, and so forth. But this would be a risky strategy, given the actors' powerful capacity to resist. Let's take a closer look at this working environment.

The first thing that stood out was the extraordinary individualism of the world of medicine. This grew out of two types of logic cohabiting within the Institution, so deeply rooted in the actors' world that no one still questioned either the reasons for their existence or the consequences of this cohabitation. Yet all these people lived together thanks only to an abundance of resources that served to paper over these contradictions. The first type of logic, which was hitherto dominant, was academic. Some of the doctors, the professors of medicine especially, were governed by this logic. For them, the methods of assessment used to determine promotions and careers were those of the academic and research worlds: this entailed publishing in 'peer-reviewed' journals, sitting on these panels, representing one's country in international learned societies, attending congresses and symposiums, and if possible presenting papers that attracted notice. This logic, which was far removed from the logic of health treatment, bred highly individualistic behaviour. The (individual) concern to manage one's career took precedence over the (collective) interest of the Institution. Anyone who has worked in the world of research has had occasion to observe this. This was due not to the doctors, who might be said to form a separate category, but to the context in which all academics and researchers functioned.

This situation had many consequences. The plainest of these was without doubt the lack of solidarity within the medical corps: it was every man for himself and God for all! At the time of the study, one of the hospitals was under threat of having its geriatric super-specialities transferred to another hospital. This prospect aroused a storm of protest, with personnel – and doctors at the forefront of this – mobilizing everything at their disposal, from the Prime Minister to celebrities with relatives or friends who had been cared for in this hospital. Colleagues in other hospitals, on the other hand, remained silent! They were indifferent or even irritated. Each stuck to his corner, fearful of being taken over by colleagues suspected of hoping to profit from the reform. But the moment an individual was not directly concerned, it was up to each person to fend for himself. As one of these unaffected doctors put it bluntly:

> *'They're crazy in this hospital. They can't imagine themselves doing the same thing elsewhere. They are behaving as if they were there by right.'*

This compartmentalized world functioned on an 'individual by individual' basis, governed by a fierce career-driven logic that was increasingly incompatible with the demands imposed by the need for a tight grip on costs. These costs presupposed cooperation and a recognition that clinical activity was as important as those activities that were currently regarded as being paramount in one's career. In a long comment, one of the interviewees analysed very clearly what this contradiction led to:

'The promotion system is highly perverse, and yet that is what determines people's future. It depends on one's publishing record, which entails a lot of travelling, going to symposiums and congresses. In fact, they spend a large amount of their paid time on it, and it doesn't matter what people say, it means one has to over-recruit in order to keep the hospital running. Nowadays, if you want to control costs without impairing quality, avoid over-prescription by the interns and pointlessly keeping people waiting until the consultant gets back, then you would risk upsetting quite a few career plans.'

A colleague confirmed this point:

'The more hospital practitioners visit the wards, the more we save in terms of the number of days spent in hospital. But in the minds of everyone, and in theirs especially, their research comes first.'

Understandably, in these conditions, any change dictated by a collective need (such as cutting costs or clearing the logjam in the accident and emergency units by taking in only the 'interesting' cases arriving) clashed with individual interests. In keeping with the doctors' logic, the logic of the 'independent professional', it was crucial to cling on to one's territory and independence, and to remain in control of one's time and work. This situation, which we have encountered elsewhere, is that of the 'marginal outsider', where one is both indispensable inside one's establishment (in this case within the Institution), while having one's own reference universe in an outside market, that of research and scientific recognition.

This made for a fragile equilibrium, and any attempt to trouble it had dramatic consequences, given the depth of divergence among the doctors. A shift in this equilibrium could not be accepted in the name of plain common sense, i.e., as the need to rationalize care, so remote was this from their concerns. Never had the dictum that common sense does not necessarily make sense been so clearly applicable. This explained why some of the arguments put forward to reject the reforms were tantamount to 'emotional terrorism': were children treated in this hospital threatened with closure really at risk of having their meal deliveries cut off? It was possible to see why public opinion had taken up the cudgels to offer the doctors unfailing support. And what about all those elderly people who were about to be abandoned in another hospital, the expiatory victims of the reforms that were then in progress? Who could put up with that?

Making the contradictory compatible

A remark is called for at this point: the world of the hospital is probably one of those where procedures are most ubiquitous. They may not always be obeyed, but they are there to ensure the patients' safety and avoid those medical mistakes that make headline news. It may come as a surprise to be asked, on entering the operating theatre, whether the organ to be operated on is well and truly the right-hand (or left-hand) one. This practice of double and triple checks only partially avoids mistakes, but it is reassuring all the same.

But these procedures were no help when it came to changing the way this hospital world functioned. Going back to what was said above, there were two contradictory logics at work in this Institution: the logic of scientific research and the logic of care. The question was how to make them compatible. This could come only through painstaking negotiation between the Institution, the doctors and the deans of the faculties that employed them. Even then, it would be necessary to interest the international scientific community in this issue, since this community held some of the keys to the problem. This would be the only way to bring the senior doctors, the professors of medicine, onside; the rule is that the higher up one is in the medical profession, the more recognition depends on the global scientific community. That is perfectly possible, and some countries have begun to recognize clinical research. But to bring everyone on board, one has no choice but to guarantee that everyone will be able to preserve their visibility, their autonomy and the control over their research necessary in order to pursue their 'work'. As we can see, the questions to be dealt with are not linear (a question, an answer), but involve actors working in different spheres. This is what sociologists call a 'concrete action system', and it takes something other than regulations or the dictates of pseudo-good sense to change it. Even then, I have simplified the picture! This is because the issue is such a hot potato that 'politicians' are constantly interfering, though theirs is the logic of 'clientelism'. One such politician was treated by a professor who now believed himself to be under threat; another was fighting the closure of a hospital unit in his constituency. In other words, this involved dealing with individuals case-by-case (e.g., the professors and politicians), while at the same time managing change in a highly complex system, provided, that is, the system had been analysed and the way in which it worked had been fully understood.

The question of room for manoeuvre

By taking the trouble to acquire detailed knowledge of the organization, one can identify possible areas for negotiation. In the present case, it was remarkable that none of the people we interviewed mentioned any personnel shortages. I had to ask the question specifically, without eliciting any particular interest on the part of interviewees. Yet this was the argument put forward most vehemently by the unions (and some politicians) in opposing the reform, virulently condemning the 'break-up' of the public hospitals. But this appeared to have no serious basis in reality, if we are to believe that 'sociological marker', the actors' spontaneous silence on a subject that their environment (the press) considered such a hot topic. None of the parties involved viewed this as a priority issue. It was being used to mobilize the public, who were always prompt to take fright at the prospect of a manpower shortage on the day they might need treatment. As one professor pointed out:

'Perhaps the question of resources is a real one, but in any case it is really complex. Healthcare workers look at what's lacking right now. But they don't want to look at the shortcomings in their organization, which could easily find additional resources from within. There are unused resources available all over the place.'

An administrative worker added:

> '*Where human resources are concerned, we have far more than the national average. Objectively, we have to reform and work more.*'

On closer inspection, this 'organizational' room for manoeuvre starts to emerge the moment a unit is threatened with the axe because it is uneconomical. Once attention turns to the unit's costs, personnel start making adjustments of their own accord by changing the organization of their work so as to reduce costs while maintaining standards of care. There is no need for appointed reformers, specialized consultants or sophisticated, pointless procedures: as in any proper negotiation, people come to see 'areas of agreement' emerging between those who want reform and those who oppose it, which merely demand to be identified and exploited. In other words, to 'grind out' a possible negotiation and break free from a sterile all-or-nothing confrontation it is necessary to work on a case-by-case basis, and not from some abstract, megalomaniac global action plan. In the case study, both those who had made this fight against the new strategy the battle of their lifetime and those far less committed actors made this point. One of the former explained this candidly:

> '*They never stop telling us we have a huge deficit. Maybe! But by reorganizing ourselves we have gone from a deficit of x million euros to one of y million. And if they left us to implement our own plan, we'd soon be on an even keel.*'

Meanwhile, one of the latter group put it this way:

> '*I told them* [the management] *to give us time to reorganize ourselves and if that – as I believe it would – allows us to gain some jobs, then there wouldn't be any problem. It's a question of time.*'

Asking for time is plainly an attempt to put back the deadline. But it also opens the way for local discussions, which, by leaving the actors concerned to sort things out, could yield considerable benefits. Instead of instituting niggling controls over the actors, the actors are put in a situation of having to control themselves. That is the difference between bureaucratic thinking and strategic thinking. And the more one tries to obtain what is hard to obtain, the less likely the bureaucratic approach is to succeed. It reassures its users, excuses them from really thinking about complexity, while enabling them to cover themselves in the event of failure. In such cases, launching a plethora of initiatives is the rule in order to shield oneself from the reproach of having done nothing, since one has indeed done everything. The final result counts for little.

That is why, in the case studied here, criticism crystallized around the method used. There is no need to be naïve here: challenging on grounds of form is always a way of shirking substantive debate. This is truer still when an awareness that something is going to have to be done some day clashes with an unwillingness to do it today. This contradiction always breeds stress and suffering. This is something one of the interviewees had understood when he said:

> '*A lot crystallizes around the method, which isn't a good one, it's true. But nobody has proposed an alternative method. That leads to an absence of counterproposals and to all kinds of tensions. In fact, we haven't been capable of devising a way of reaching consensus. Now we're paying for it.*'

This should not be taken at face value. No one denied that focusing on the 'how' served to avoid a discussion of 'what'. But things were never entirely black and white, and it was the way in which the Institution arrived at its decisions that opened the door to this pirouette.

This may seem paradoxical insofar as this Institution comprised numerous local and central bodies, involving a not inconsiderable number of people. Moreover, no one seriously contested their existence or their mode of operation. This simply pointed the finger at another form of managerial sloth: in this type of organization, and in many others, meetings quickly turn into a routine. The actors attend because they 'represent' a particular part of the organization and because, politically, it is normal that they should be represented. The issues on the agenda are of unequal interest to those present, but everyone emerges satisfied, if only because they have filled half a day. Interestingly, the people who complain that these meetings 'are pointless' call for just as many meetings as the others. This is a ritual in organizations, and presumably it plays a socializing role, which after all is not to be sneered at. Moreover, the first thing those attending look at is who is there and who is not.

However, when tension rises, rituals cease to function. In the present case, faced with the tension and concerns engendered by a change that had been announced yet had never been implemented, but which all of a sudden materialized, the procedures of informing, consulting and involving people needed to go far beyond what took place in the official bodies. To give an example of such a scenario, when Air France was grappling with the problems mentioned earlier, the Chairman, who had been appointed in difficult circumstances, took the time to 'build' the necessary knowledge, in spite (or perhaps because) of a situation demanding urgent measures. But then, in order to devise and gain acceptance to solutions, some of them unpalatable to the actors concerned, the method employed was highly 'inclusive'. Ad hoc task forces were formed, comprised of people selected not on the basis of short-term political considerations but because they were stakeholders in a 'complex sequence' representing a substantial portion of what constituted quality as perceived by the client. Subsequently, management's role was to validate (or not) the suggestions that flowed from these proceedings. There was nothing formal or artificial in this, but, and to revert to one of the central themes of this book, it was a question of mutual trust.

In the case study, one of the 'decision makers'(!) made the opposite observation:

> *'It's true, we hadn't really communicated about what we were doing. So people had no general vision and felt excluded. There was a real problem of inadequate explanation.'*

But while this can be taken as a minimalist self-criticism, all of the actors confirmed this view, including the administrative staff, many of which were responsible for implementing the project:

> *'Our plan was not presented in sufficiently objective terms. As a result, major decisions were taken in the absence of facts and figures to explain on what basis and to justify what was about to be done. Things broke down because of that. People know there has to be change, but they don't know on what basis the decisions will be taken.'*

Clearly, the absence of any clearly stated meaning behind the reforms constantly fed the rumour mill and fears over their consequences, placing an artificial obstacle in the way of acceptance of the change taking place and undercutting potential support. A hospital manager, one of the people who might have served as a link in the deployment of the reform, noted:

> *'Most of the doctors were not hostile to the reforms. But they want to be listened to in a clear framework, and that isn't exactly the case today.'*

Here again, the system effect is striking: what rendered the local administrative staff all the more helpless in the face of the actors' concerns and pressures was that they were in daily contact with the latter, but the actors' messages were unclear and hasty, offering no real sense of their likely impact. Hardly surprisingly, in this situation of 'strategic destitution', the actors opted to play 'local' versus 'the central'. As in any change process, how things were done took precedence over what was done, hence the recurring criticisms of the 'method' employed, which ended up isolating those who made the decisions from any possible support they might have had. This is how one hospital manager put it:

> *'Where the project is concerned, people see only parts of it. People can listen to and understand that the Institution needs to reform, and even to shut down establishments. But the method is unacceptable. We know nothing about the impact of these restructurings on the personnel, even if we understand that the Institution is not in control of everything and of all the decisions. We know some of these are taken elsewhere.'*

It is worth listening to a number of interview excerpts to see that this 'cry' was springing up everywhere. It should also be borne in mind that management alone was not to blame for this collective frustration – far from it. Much of it also flowed from the constraints surrounding the Institution, which came from outside but which it was obliged to handle internally. So sensitive was the issue of reforming the Institution (the role of politicians was noted previously) that everyone was seeking to take control over communicating their own logic, which had nothing to do with the issue of change management.

Even internally, the project's designers had been so conscious of likely opposition to it that they delayed talking about it until the last possible moment, even if, ultimately, that meant doing so clumsily. As so often happens, each person believes other people are predictable, develops complex assumptions about their possible reactions, then abandons the field of reality in favour of conspiracy theories and ends up creating the very conditions leading to the fulfilment of his pessimistic forecasts – a self-fulfilling prophecy. We are right in the thick of one here!

Obviously it was not easy to turn around this tendency towards mistrust and caution, which guaranteed the present moment at the expense of the final outcome. The entire 'mechanism' put in motion was hard to reverse: most of the actors – and among them many of those that 'count' – were far more receptive to change than its designers, who lived isolated and barricaded in anticipation of an assault that never materialized, had imagined. Quite simply, the different actors demanded clarity, trust, coherence, foresight and management of the consequences. But the managers' negative expectations made these hard to implement. Added to this was this organization's bureaucratic tradition whereby, barring a handful of managers, 'head office' had lost sight of its strategic mission and had become bogged down in the minutiae of everyday administration. A member of the central administrative staff put it clearly:

> *'The staff functions at head office are in no position to manage change. They're bogged down in the details. They have neither the time nor the tools to manage change, and in addition they don't trust the hospitals.'*

The need for go-betweens

We need to go a step further, now, to understand just how hard it is to win back lost ground in these organizations that have 'let everything slip' and which under pressure from their environment now want to execute a U-turn. Let us start by noting that the above account illustrates a famous paradox: here was an organization that for years had been 'self-managed' by its members and that was now faced with an awkward situation bereft of either proper consultation channels or adequate means for involving personnel in its decisions. In other words, 'self-management' worked well as a means of distributing abundant resources; it was less appropriate for dealing with difficulties. It needed to change its practices and to adapt them to a hitherto unfamiliar situation, based on a precise understanding of the needs and aspirations of the different actors concerned.

Given that the traditional consultation channels had 'blown up', the first need was to find 'go-betweens', people capable of supporting initiatives taken, explaining them and above all able to deal with its individual and collective impacts on a daily basis. In the case of this Institution, executives from the central administration and/or the hospital managers could play this role. By establishing a permanent dialogue between central logic and local logic, this 'ideal' approach should have assisted in breaking out of the syndrome of decisions announced at the last minute and thus kept the rumour mill and accusations of ulterior motives in check. But the present situation within the Institution was a far cry from this. There were plenty of people who supported the reforms, but they were scattered throughout the organization, did not talk to each other and consequently did not amount to a force that could counted upon.

Meanwhile, support for the reforms at 'head office' was lukewarm, to put it mildly: many of the executives there had made their career in hospital management. They were stakeholders in what this category called – without a hint of a pejorative connotation – 'the corporatism of the hospital managers'. The moment this category felt itself under attack, rightly or wrongly, its response was a corporatist one, as its name suggests. A head office executive put it this way:

> *'Investment problems lie behind some of the closures. But I have grave doubts about closing establishments, with one exception. In fact, we're far from convinced, at head office, as to the rationale behind some aspects of the reform. Creating eight hospital clusters, for instance* [a key aspect of this reform], *is a monstrous mistake in terms of organization and administration. It will lead to cost over-runs and negative outcomes.'*

A hospital manager echoed this point:

> *'The project started out on principles we said were impossible. The project was based on technocratic principles, and we know they don't work. In fact, there were several reforms that telescoped, creating terrible confusion.'*

And yet this situation was not unavoidable. Some hospital managers had gone along with the reforms. As might be expected, these were managers who benefited from the reforms, those who had been made managers of hospital clusters. So did others who had the feeling they were being involved in the changes affecting their establishments. The problem was, quite simply, that the approach taken was so erratic that, once again, it yielded piecemeal effects. All these people became good go-betweens, committing themselves to the day-to-day business of dealing with critical problems and doing all they could to assist with the smooth deployment of the reform. One of them noted:

> *'In my establishment, head office's plans aren't unreasonable, especially as I helped frame them. But I don't want to be trapped, as at Hospital X. I'm proceeding slowly and deliberately, so that little by little the medical staff buys into the project. It's an interesting process in the end.'*

Thus, it is possible to avoid finding oneself in a position of being alone against all. It is possible to make allies, to harness them in the pursuit of intelligent strategies of step-by-step negotiations, to seize opportunities as they arise while keeping the overall project in mind. But in order for this to work, there was one last condition that had until this point escaped the notice of this Institution, which was obsessed with the need to drive 'change', i.e., 'we want it all and we want it now'. Observation showed that, in this case, to speak of 'the' project or 'the' reform is misleading. In fact, there were several reforms in progress that were colliding with each other, to the great relief of those who did not want any reform. There was *medical reform*, no doubt the trickiest and the one attracting the widest media coverage, which consisted of combining units, merging them or transferring them. Its opponents were highly capable of mobilizing outside support. Alongside this was *administrative reform*, itself split in two: part of it concerned the creation of hospital clusters, while the other part concerned cutting the bloated numbers of head office staff. No wonder, then, that opening up all these 'fronts' in no clear order of priority should have undermined the chances of success of each of its parts. Management found itself doing battle with 'coalitions of interests' that it had itself engendered, without at the same time rallying its supporters, who remained scattered across all four corners of the battlefield. Opposition crystallized, intermediaries grew weary and the chances of success dwindled.

It is plain to see where the difficulty comes from when trying to change such self-centred organizations, where management and supervisory authorities (where the latter exist) alike have consistently bowed to pressure. Their problem has been not so much an absence of procedures or control mechanisms (they are there aplenty), but the disappearance of the simple norms of collective life. Added to this initial detachment from 'real life' is the absence of comparison with the outside world, which makes it hard to realize that ordinary situations that no longer surprise anyone are in fact outrageous: working time, long holidays and high levels of absenteeism have little by little permeated the normal functioning of the organization. The cost of all of this is nobody's business, and management buys peace on the labour front, assuming itself to be under constant threat (the famous 'fear of labour unrest'). Employees, meanwhile, fail to see where the problem is, since resources are always in short supply, whatever happens.

In this kind of configuration, one needs to burn what formerly one adored in order to bring about sometimes painful changes. Where virtual self-management used to be seen as an open and modern(!) form of staff-management dialogue, people end up acting undercover, planning decisions in small committees, practising a 'land grab' strategy: you grab from 'them' whatever you can, when you can, which merely ends up legitimizing and nurturing the initial mistrust, which in turn bolsters the preference for acting in secret. This is the routine tale of non-change in endogenous bureaucracies. I repeat that, even though this was not the purpose of this book, I wanted to show that possibilities do exist for doing things differently. As for being listened to ...

8
Simplicity, Trust and Communities of Interest: Can Things Be Done Differently?

The day-to-day life of companies is not just a matter of processes spinning in a void, ineffectual controls or all-devouring intermediate bureaucracies. Different organizations have opted for different choices, without necessarily being able to explain why. A simple deterministic view might lead to the conclusion that they found themselves in different situations in different markets at different points in time. But that is not so, as we shall see in the examples that follow. Similarly, explanations in terms of history are as attractive as they are unsatisfactory. All of the companies visited, with the notable exception of those in the public sector, had experienced a phase of entrepreneurship, during which 'doing' took precedence over the question of 'how'. In most cases, they then 'rationalized' how they did things in ways that form the raw material of this book. This vision, based on 'phases of development', is attractive because it is Cartesian. In addition, it enables a healthy fatalism in the face of what we know to be pointless (the plethora of processes and controls), without having the means or will to remedy this. This is but a short step from saying one might as well just wait for things to blow over. But, as we have seen, things only blow over (if indeed they ever do) under heavy pressure from the organization's environment.

Yet this explanation is unsatisfactory, since many companies have not experienced this phase of standardization, and voices are now being raised advising them to not to do so.[1] I shall come back to this in my conclusion. Suffice it to say, for the time being, that companies manage to preserve their early flexibility and turn this into a 'key to success'. No doubt their chief executive or top executives are instrumental in preserving this wisdom. And if we were to rein in all that hollow talk about leaders and leadership, no doubt we could serenely ponder the following observation: a chief executive is all the stronger when he trusts, and the stronger he is, the more he trusts. Trust is precisely what I have been holding up in this book in opposition to procedure-laden bureaucracy. One needs to be sure of oneself, of the people one has picked and above all of the ground rules one has established in one's organization in order to be confident that all this will foster a mode of operation which, while less reassuring perhaps, is more effective than what is described in the management textbooks.

This helps us to understand that the 'moment of truth' for a company is indeed the moment of transition from a founding father or charismatic leader to a 'standardized' management. This is because working in a 'fuzzy' organization, and even more so running one, is something one has to be able to 'feel', and those capable of doing so are not in the majority – far from it. The new managers want to put things in order as soon as they arrive, to get a grip on things, redefine roles and introduce clarity, and the consultants are there to help them. I shall not return to the question of what then happens in practice. I keenly remember a large electronic equipment manufacturer – not in our sample – whose youthful new boss, after applying these rules of sound management and producing the human results that ensued, appointed a senior executive to 'restore entrepreneurship'. He did what he could, i.e., not much. The financial results were good to begin with, but the atmosphere deteriorated to the point where the head of human resources (HR) – who had merely expressed his disagreement, in vain – was fired and replaced.

We will now discuss the examples of three organizations that tried to 'do things differently'. I have chosen them because they are very different from each other, not just to avoid being accused of picking organizations whose situations are too similar, but also to show that there are choices all the time. Managements that justify their choices on grounds of determinism display a lack of imagination at best, and at worst are confessing their failure. For these final case studies, I shall again try to avoid being naïve or Manichean. In order to do so, I am going to have to identify the limits as to what these companies these can do, whenever the occasion arises, showing what is possible and when they can attempt to do it, within the context of their existing 'culture'.

Let's start with the case of a major West Coast logistics company in the United States.[2] It was large enough to be a global operator, albeit with a pronounced China bias, given its location. Its structure was simple, with a small headquarters in the Los Angeles suburbs and branches scattered worldwide, which were very loosely organized around countries and regions. Three salient features emerged from my observations of its daily operations.

The first was the company's firmly entrenched sense of teamwork at all levels. As many interviewees told us, 'There's no room for egos here' or (this is the United States, after all) 'We're looking for rock groups, not rock stars'. I must point out right away that this 'anti-star' obsession is a hallmark of firms in the United States, encapsulated in the famous remark by Jack Welch:[3] 'We like wild ducks, provided they fly in formation.' By way of contrast, Michel Crozier pointed to the 'individualism with anarchic tendencies' that characterizes French culture.

Regulation,[4] not rules

Underlying these strong statements in this company was the fact that the actors were heavily dependent on each other. This had nothing to do with rules or procedures, nor with any kind of system of control, but simply with the fact that, given the way in which the company ran its operations, if one part of the organization under-performed, then this had immediate repercussions on another part of it: one branch dispatched, another received. Whatever one employee did in his position facilitated or threatened the work, results and pay of someone else.

The company could be considered to be self-regulating in that respect. If it proved necessary to sanction someone, the demand emanated not only from management but also from that person's peers; as such, there was no chance of a culture of 'me, myself and I' arising. No one could win on their own in this organization, against others or in spite of them, but with them and with their help. One of the remarkable features of this was the juxtaposition of this very high degree of dependence between the local branches – the key actors in this system, in fact – with the fact that they did not know each other and practically never met. Informal practice was the watchword. There was no need for an endless round of meeting, trips and working sessions: everyone knew the 'rules of the game' and used them efficiently. The head office had understood this well and had 'positioned' its own staff functions as 'in-house consultants'. These interfered very little in local activities and trust was so tightly integrated as a mode of interaction between all of the actors that the others would instantly sanction the slightest breach or betrayal.

As we can see, this situation is a far cry from such conventional management clichés as: 'the closer the offices are to each other, the better people work together', 'people need to know each other for trust to grow' and 'scattered activities demand stronger processes'. No: the question is not one of rules, but of regulation, of the way the different actors were induced to adjust their strategies to fit those of others and had no choice but to act collectively or risk rejection by this virtual community.

However, at the time that this study was being conducted, voices were starting to be raised at headquarters to suggest that 'sure, this isn't a top-down company, but all the same ...', suggesting that there *might* be some limits to this local freedom. This was a clear signal that some management circles were starting to contemplate the need to build a more integrated company. Their reason, though vague, was the imminent retirement of the last founders, which chimes with our initial hypothesis regarding the moment of transition from 'founding father' to 'standardized' management.

A second characteristic was the small role played by rules, procedures and processes. Not only were there few of them, but those that did exist were based on a strict principle of universally accepted necessity. In any case, everyone created their own rules, as for example in the case of the management tools used by the local managers. Each person felt entitled to create his own key indicators; if these proved to be worthwhile, they stood a good chance of gaining acceptance by the rest of the company. Generally speaking, this local management considered that the oversight was flexible(!) and that it had full control over its unit. One of them told us 'here, the succession plan depends on me alone' and everyone approved, arguing that this was what made the job interesting.

Even more surprisingly, the actors acknowledged that this firm encouraged 'overlaps'. Now this was an unusual position, quite contradictory to the principles of sound management, which posits that two people doing the same thing cost more than if just one person does it. This pseudo-common sense implies that functions and duties need to be clearly defined. Frontiers between individuals, departments, units, etc., must be totally unambiguous in order to avoid duplication. In fact, all this is artificial, since this fascination with clarity leads to the emergence of internal monopolies, which behave inside the organization like any monopoly in a market. They make the rest of the organization pay the price for their monopolistic situation. Readers have merely to observe relations between an IT department and the rest of a company to grasp this simple mechanism. That is precisely what the company in the case study being discussed here had been trying diligently to avoid.

The third curiosity regarding this supply-chain firm was the importance of networks in the day-to-day running of the company. Perhaps unsurprisingly in so fuzzy an organization, it was very important to know the 'right people'. This was the best way to deal with any problem, and indeed this was consistent with the absence of procedures. Everyone said 'I know who to go to for the help I need', which reinforced the need to play very much as a team and to alternate naturally between stints in the branches and at headquarters.

To conclude this brief analysis, it is worth noting the implicit trade-off in this organization that gave it its effectiveness, namely that it fostered a high degree of autonomy at the local level as long as it made for a high level of efficiency. This allowed local actors to keep their distance from headquarters staff and to 'use' the latter only when needed, and it was they who determine the frequency and intensity of relations. Again, this was consistent with the headquarters executives who defined themselves as consultants, which would come as a surprise in a more integrated outfit. Better still, it was the head office executives who most readily emphasized the very heavy workload of the people 'on the ground', describing their role as being to minimize any disruption they might cause in the work of the local actors.

Does this mean that everything was fine? Surely not, and it is worth mentioning certain questions that were now surfacing in this company, *without, however, considering their emergence inevitable*, as we will demonstrate in the third case study given later in this chapter. Nevertheless, it is worth noting that this organization was totally dependent on the people comprising it. When asked about what might be a problem for them, all our interviewees spoke in terms of people: one had resigned, another had to be disciplined, yet another wanted to move – all this formed part of the overriding daily concerns. This system could endure for as long as the top managers agreed to this method of managing people on a 'case-by-case' basis and did not feel the need to bring everything under control. Whatever the case, this company's rapid growth, combined with the departure of its founder, will very likely lead to the ground rules being spelt out more thoroughly, laying down what is acceptable and what is not, and what is and is not negotiable.

This was especially true inasmuch as the mode of operation we have just observed was atypical compared to other companies. It owed its legitimacy to the founder; he made it acceptable to work in this unconventional way, paving the way for the firm's success. His successor would no doubt have to stabilize the odd 'cornerstone' in the organization, while avoiding the risk of bureaucracy, lurking in the woods ready to spring out at the first opportunity. Introducing greater formalization (which was not the case at the time of this study) was the leader's dilemma. History is now in the making.

The bureaucracy of experts

Now for a change of continent and for a look at an environment more surprising still in many respects. This case study combines both the classic features of bureaucracies, a great deal of efficiency in terms of its results and some questions as to its capacity to do things differently in order to adapt to the changing demands of its clients. It involves an employers' organization, representing a major sector of the country's economy.[5] True, at first glance the image that sprung to mind, at least for the head office, which dominated the local and industry bodies, was that of a cumbersome, hierarchy-ridden, rigid and endogenous bureaucracy. It continued imperturbably to churn out ever more complicated and arcane legal documents. It was surrounded by a 'periphery' expressing a high degree of satisfaction with the services it provided, respectful of the sophisticated expertise of those working at head office and reluctant to challenge the legal experts' dominance.

In other words, this organization's clients were satisfied with it, provided their demands remained within the 'parent organization's' area of competence. This was a remarkable state of affairs and there was nothing automatic about it: bureaucracies rarely prompt applause from those using them! As such, it is worth trying to understand how novel, effectively 'customer-driven' modes of operation came into being, with their primary emphasis on informality, flexibility and responsiveness. It is faintly amusing to note that these people, so highly specialized in analysing and writing rules and procedures, had been careful not to impose any on themselves when it came to defining how they worked, and above all how they worked together. This was almost a textbook case.

To say this institution was 'expertise-driven' would be an understatement, since expertise here was cultivated, upheld and venerated. This was hardly surprising, since it protected the autonomy of those that possessed it. This accounted for the long years of learning essential to acquiring expertise and no doubt the overrating of the amount of time it took to do so. This was verging on 'legal aestheticism', which explained why the holders of these different forms of expertise found it practically impossible to glimpse possible successors. Even then, some expressed doubts as to their real degree of competence:

> *'Where competencies are concerned, for the first year you don't even know what you are doing. After five years you have some vague idea. After ten years, it's OK, and you can still be stumped even after 20 years.'*

> *'When you've been there 20 years, you at last manage to answer 95 per cent of the questions you get asked without having to get up.'*

> *'No ... I don't know how my work is assessed ... as long as there are no complaints ... everyone seems content. And yet, my director doesn't seem to realize that, compared to him, I still have gaps in my knowledge.'*

Not surprisingly, this super-expertise bred bureaucratic habits that were easy to list, including: a predominantly magisterial tendency that paid little heed to whatever did not form part of the narrow scope of the official's legal specialization; an organization where nobody knew why it functioned as it did, particularly with regard to the departmental distribution of areas of competence, although everyone considered it intangible and immutable. The following quote is an amusing illustration of this:

> *'Work time and labour conflicts? No, it's got nothing to do with it. I don't know how it came about. It hasn't changed since I started here, 26 years ago. But it's the same for the other departments.'*

There was very little mobility between these departments. Nor did the actors want mobility. Everyone had the sense of being in an exceptional, protective 'cocoon', especially when compared to the other departments (of which they knew practically nothing). Again, the organization functioned like a 'honeycomb', in a fashion more like that of administrative organizations: each employee felt part of a special community, focused on his area of competence corresponding to a part of the labour code; the degree to which each employee was allowed to interact with the environment was hierarchical in the extreme, each person being aware of the rank of the persons he was entitled to address. This implicit rule allowed the directors to maintain total control over their sphere, over what it produced and hence over its image in the eyes of clients and the rest of the institution. An interviewee described things as follows:

> *'Relations with top brass are not simple, and in fact, we have no relations at all. We ought to be more closely involved with our superiors, but the top managers only talk to the departmental heads, never to us. And the directors themselves only talk to their counterparts.'*

In fact, there was a very high degree of organizational 'immaturity'. This was reflected in the place subjective feelings had come to occupy in relations, a little as if these could sometimes substitute for the customary rigidity of relations. An interviewee had this to say:

> *'People here mix their personal and professional lives. Many take things personally. Things the boss says can be blown up to enormous proportions. Nobody has the slightest detachment from all this, which leads to dramas.'*

This first-level observation marks a welcome return to the start of this book: here is another of these compartmentalized organizations, withdrawn into themselves, insensitive to the needs and demands of their customers, in this case its regional entities. And yet they are satisfied? As such, there must be a second level of interpretation to allow us to understand this paradox: how can an endogenous bureaucracy provide service to a level of quality that no one disputes?

One might think that the client – who happened to be captive in this case – had understood what he can expect from this organization and had adjusted his expectations accordingly. The resulting virtuous circle had reinforced the institution's unrivalled expertise. Why not? The trouble was that this explanation ignored a more complex reality, namely that this organization had evolved flexible, informal modes of operation that enabled it to respond swiftly and effectively to the demands of its environment, though still within its hyper-specialized confines.

Even a bureaucracy can be flexible

Going further, let's now see what it was that so greatly satisfied the members of this employers' union. Everyone acknowledged its capacity to 'give rulings on the law', including those that produced the law, namely the specialized government departments. As one of its legal experts pointed out:

> *'Companies and our territorial units are highly satisfied with the services we provide. We have often rectified errors made by their lawyers or even by government departments.'*

Needless to say, the degree of pressure exerted on these specialists varied according to the area concerned and the urgency with which answers were required. Anything relating to the handling of disputes, dismissals and redundancy plans was highly sensitive, but employment contracts and collective agreements were less so. Some of the nuances in assessments of the assistance furnished stemmed from that fact. Similarly, examining these subtleties further, we find that the 'raw' legal department, the department that dealt with the application or immediate interpretation of the law, was more highly appreciated than the department concerned with producing more analytical documents. This stemmed from the absence of delegation mentioned earlier: the boss wanted to control everything coming out of his department. This limited the amount of material that could be produced for the 'market'. Choices therefore had to be made, and the first to be sacrificed was the 'political' interpretation of legal texts, the employers' doctrine as it were. Moreover, the adverse side-effects of this centralization were clearly perceived on the ground. A representative of a regional body made the following point:

> *'I'd like to be informed about the political viewpoints on a number of issues. We need to think about communicating orally more quickly and*

more openly. Sometimes they [at head office] *are reluctant to put certain things in writing, for whatever reason.'*

However, having run the gamut of nuances, the striking thing was this remarkable capacity to harness the array of expertise needed to produce rapid and precise answers to complex questions. In fact, this performance was down to the informal way in which the organization operated, allied to an implicit rule that a response would be provided for any request whatever via spontaneous cooperation among the actors. Together, these framed an 'integrated' argument, which was then communicated to the person making the request. In other words, this organization was remarkably skilful at breaking through its segmented, compartmentalized routine to satisfy the demands of its clients. And the paradox within a paradox, what made this open behaviour possible, was another rule whereby no one ever encroached on another's turf. What a telling example of how to sow the seeds of trust by reducing behavioural uncertainty! Once this was clear to all, there was no need for anyone to feel threatened when calling on a wide range of expertise in order to answer the most complex questions – and there were many of them.

This remarkable 'customer focus' had emerged through 'fuzziness', not via rules, procedures and processes. This was an undeniably original form of know-how, reflecting a degree of flexibility and responsiveness few organizations could match. Indeed, the actors involved were well aware of these practices:

'We work in a fair degree of isolation, day-to-day. That's true. But we are able to work as a team on questions we are unable to answer single-handed. And it's the same thing between departments. Maybe we are compartmentalized, but it's informal. We are perfectly capable of working together.'

'The work is shared out in a highly informal manner. Me, for example, I am in charge of monitoring the Journal Officiel, *and then we apportion the work informally. We have departmental and inter-departmental meetings, all equally informal, whenever the need arises or in case of difficulty.'*

'We get on very well with the legal people in the other departments. We call each other in order to answer our members. We have a good idea of our colleagues' sphere of competence.'

In other organizations, these would be called 'virtual communities'. We will come back to this later on. It is worth pointing out, for the time being, that this fuzzy approach to day-to-day business unsurprisingly featured in the management of personnel. Here again, the more senior legal experts on rules had successfully avoided having their hands tied by the constraints they daily urged on others. There was no personnel representation, for example, and the mere mention of it struck everyone as incongruous. Nor was there any careers management either or clear criteria for evaluating performance, awarding pay rises or any other question relating to the administration of personnel. In short, this was an aristocracy, one that exempted itself from what it imposed on its client-subjects. Everything was done informally, through face-to-face relations, and above all in the very real trust between the boss and 'his' legal experts. The latter had this to say:

> *'No one evaluates me ... no ... maybe by word of mouth, but in any case there's no formalized process. But evaluating people who have been there 20 years would probably go down badly.'*

> *'Perhaps we would like an evaluation interview. What we have is an informal one. We have no idea on what basis pay increases are decided. Many things take place informally, and it's always worked very well like that.'*

Therefore, no one was complaining, or at least not officially. But it could not be overlooked that some had jumped ship: those that didn't fit in, feeling ill at ease in a mode of operation as impressionistic as this. In those cases, the institution acted (positively) as a first-class training ground for youngsters who could later sell their skills to the highest bidder. This left those able to find their way around this peculiar universe, who had understood its customs and mores, and who were then able to reproduce this mode of operation and pass it on. This process of acculturation helped to account for the longevity of this universe, but the learning process was a long one.

The organization was an attractive one in many respects and was one of the keys to the success of its institution, representing a clear competitive advantage. However, it had its limitations. It was well suited to precise requests, ones that were familiar and standardized. This meant that there was a risk of it becoming confined to this role at a time when clients were diversifying their demands and when its foreign counterparts were experimenting with a much more varied array of services. The regional entities themselves were taking initiatives to go beyond the purely legal sphere. These were proactive initiatives, with entities seeking to develop new areas of competence, hiring people from outside the legal professions, and the new recruits were launching out into supply-side policies, addressing needs their employers had yet to formalize. This is how two of the new recruits described their approach:

> *'Employers are grappling with new problems. For example, they ought to have begun long ago to expand their thinking beyond their local area. But they haven't taken into account this aspect of globalization and nor have we. We reply in purely legal terms, as experts. But we need to think harder about the human resources dimension, about new competencies, and strategy, etc.'*

> *'We create links between firms, by sector, in order to mount economic development projects. We run networks and above all we manage projects. We need to keep a permanent watch on each industry sector. For example, I bring in a large firm so that subcontractors are properly informed about what is going on and can adjust to the new purchasing criteria.'*

Once this new offer came into existence and entered the local entities' 'basket' of offers, it triggered a wave of demands, especially amid the worsening economic situation. What was emerging was a progressive inversion of the dominant logic, which was still that of the institution, namely waiting for (exclusively legal) questions to arrive, then mobilizing resources on a formidable scale in order to answer them. This was a reactive posture, making complex knowledge available to those requesting it. What was emerging at the local level (and in other comparable countries) was something very different: this involved 'looking for questions', anticipating, helping firms to formalize their present and future needs. These needs had far more to do with the economic sphere than with labour issues, the latter having been narrowed down to the application of employment law.

Two further remarks are called for regarding the strategies developed by the local entities, once more leading us into a systemic logic. These entities were utilizing the institution's long-established legitimacy in the field of employment law to forge their own legitimacy in new areas; they were responding vigorously to growing competition in the field of business services. In order to do this, they were leveraging the quasi-family nature of relations between member companies and the institution as a whole. In a nutshell, local entities were 'capturing' the institution's image and relationships for their own benefit, 'bypassing' the latter in the services they provided. The wheel will have come full circle if we can understand what they could expect from their parent organization in these conditions. In fact, they did not expect all that much and there was a considerable temptation to maintain the institution in its current role. Doubts were emerging more or less everywhere regarding its capacity to adopt more innovative forms of action, with a greater emphasis on taking the lead and rapidly turning out more forward-looking analyses, as opposed to 'interpretive' ones. Given these doubts, local units were increasingly networking among themselves, to the exclusion of the centre. This enabled them to pool ideas and experiences, as well as human resources they would be unable to draw on acting in isolation.

For the time being, these networks were being formed on an ad hoc basis, according to needs and circumstances. The initiatives were still very local, depending on the extent to which local officials were inspired to cast their recruitment net more widely. As such, for now, this did not add up to a policy, but it was on its way to becoming one. The parent organization would soon have to confront the question as to its capacity to break out of its present well-oiled and efficient but narrowly focused routine. In order to do so, it would need to retain the informal modes of cooperation that had given it its legitimacy in the specific area of law, while acquiring new capabilities, even though managing these would no doubt entail sacrificing some of its traditional modes of operation. This will doubtless not be a matter of *either-or* but of *both together*, and its success will depend on the capacity to strike a happy medium between the two for as long as possible.

The complexity of organizations

Once again, I must point out that our picture of life in organizations has grown more complex as this journey has unfolded: we cannot speak of endogenous bureaucracies on the one hand, applauding their early demise, in contrast to the flexibility and responsiveness of market sector companies on the other hand. Not only is the opposition not reducible to this simplistic Manichaean vision, but above all these two modes of operation (and probably others too) coexist within the same organizations. Private bureaucracies are no better than public ones, and bureaucratic flexibility is just as worthy as the flip-flops of certain companies in their response to managerial fads.

What we are starting to perceive, in fact, is that the difference revolves around *simplicity*.[6] This embraces the simplicity of relationships, of 'structures', of forms of collective working – everything that allows us to do things quickly, well and cheaply. But simplicity does not mean clarity: little is 'clear' in collective life, hence the reference to that terrorist, manipulative notion of transparency: 'Tell me everything and I will tell you nothing.' Simplicity implies knowing what is doable and what is not, shortening circuits where needed and creating virtual groups as required, with no need for political arrangements (who should we bring in to avoid hurting anyone's feelings?) and without this group enduring indefinitely after completing its mission. This is why integration is not coterminous with process, but with simplicity and rules of the game.

Not surprisingly, then, our final case study takes us to a company that had probably been the most successful out of the companies examined in the case studies in integrating, and had succeeded in making it last, notwithstanding a long list of acquisitions and the vicissitudes of the market.

I have had several occasions to observe this major cosmetics firm over the past 20 years. On the last occasion (this is the study discussed here),[7] its managers took care to ensure that their young executives, drawn from all over the world, understood this firm's special modes of operation (its culture), knowing that it was not easy to adapt to it. I therefore had to compare the present-day organization with that of yesterday, and I recall having titled the memorandum I submitted on that occasion: 'The Culture of X: not many differences, a great deal of continuity, for the same performance.'

True, this question of 'culture' (an organization's recurring practices and behaviours) had consistently been central to this company. And indeed it was highly atypical: its somewhat unorthodox nature came as a surprise when set beside the canons of modern management. Yet the company had performed impressively, in economic terms, year after year. This suggested there was a close and direct link between the way it functioned on a day-to-day basis, tackled problems and took decisions, and its financial results. This was also true of its human results: as we shall see in the following paragraphs, life there could be very tough, but the 'brand's' power of attraction remained intact, placing it at the top of future executives' list of desirable firms to work for.

This working culture had always been portrayed as 'fuzzy' (we are now starting to have an idea what this means), where flowcharts, job descriptions, rules and procedures had been treated as secondary or even banned outright. This firm had consistently preferred 'confrontation', its favourite word, albeit somewhat less flaunted today, to a written, codified, clear organization. Similarly, there were many 'overlaps' between functions, which were treated as normal for reasons I have explored already in this work, and which this company was almost alone in having embraced and above all incorporated into its 'management principles'. One interviewee found a telling formula to explain this:

> 'We do not function in project mode, or at least not in a formal way, as always in this firm. When work is organized by projects there is always a leader. Here, there are always several leaders, and things work well that way.'

Again, this must not be taken at face value: this fuzziness never extended to the production side, which would never have tolerated it. However, it had consistently been the hallmark of relations between R&D, marketing and sales. What is more – and this is surely the hardest thing to explain – this fuzziness no doubt illustrated the permanent misunderstanding surrounding this company's 'customer focus'. Viewed from a traditional angle, this company could be seen as being 'product-driven'. And it was true that companies in this sector, at the luxury end especially, had a natural tendency to think that their 'brands' drove the market far more than the other way round. But in reality it is worth asking which took precedence (in the positive sense) in this never-ending standoff, in the complex and highly political business of handing these 'overlaps' between countries, brands, regions and divisions. Knowledge of the market, of 'its' market, is what allows a company to commit to a result, with all of the possible repercussions, of course, if it gets things wrong. 'Winning' demands more than mere talk; one must also be able to do.

So much for the general background, against which generations of employees, executives and top managers have lived their careers. But had this culture stood the test of time, mergers and successive crises, not to mention changes of chief executives and the attendant strategic shifts? Or had it been forced to 'get back in line' and revert to managerial norms closer to those taught in reputable business schools? As we shall see, while there had been changes, imposed as always by the environment, these had been very marginal and had only occurred at a superficial level. At the heart, though, continuity has prevailed.

When asked about what had changed in the company since their arrival, none of the interviewees mentioned the way it did things on a day-to-day basis. For them, things had always been the same! Yet, on closer inspection, it was possible to identify areas where change was undeniable: HR management had been put on a more professional footing, for example, a subject we will return to later in this discussion, and relations between marketing and research were more cordial and trusting than had previously been the case.

However, this was not the most interesting aspect: everyone agreed that the competition was becoming increasingly fierce, while distributors were better and better organized, putting constant pressure on prices. No one had the slightest doubt that the company was standing up to all this. But it was doing so by boosting productivity, which boiled down to asking all of its employees to work harder. However, it had left its mode of operation untouched. In other words, contrary to what we have observed in most cases, the company's organization had not served as the adjustment variable in response to the modern-day demand for 'more and more for less and less'. Neither pressure from the financial markets nor the massive influx of activities from an English-speaking world with little love for fuzziness had left a deep and lasting impact on the 'core' of this very special environment. It had remained alive (though not immutable); everyone had learned to sustain it in their own fashion, adapting to it, even if that took time and entailed setbacks. It is therefore necessary to take a closer look at this environment in order to seek insight into those characteristics that together formed a 'system'. These can be grouped together around a handful of broad themes.

A culture of confrontation

Behind the company's 'structures', which had grown increasingly complex as a result of the impact of expanding territories and product lines, the terms of the 'confrontation' remained the same. The word itself came up again and again, like a leitmotif, in conversations with interviewees, yet none of them used it in a pejorative sense. One gave this 'timeless' description of everyday life:

> *'It's the region* [one of the new structures] *that is now between a rock and a hard place. It's in permanent confrontation with the brand. The brand has a global logic, by definition, but the regions can argue about their need to develop. Similarly, there's a confrontation over the brand image: you can't use the same visual everywhere. The region may ask for care to be taken, and it's the same for the notion of services, which aren't equally important everywhere.'*

This gave rise to a highly 'political' way of doing things (as opposed to one driven by procedures), which resolved differences of opinion and (above all) interests. These factors worked hand-in-hand. Both were part of the everyday routine, as one interviewee put it:

> *'There's a lot of politics here, and we spend our time cleaning up after false alerts. And that's why I can't describe our organization to you: it's much too political.'*

> *'It's all really very complex, because this company is a matrix organization in the full sense of the term, with numerous entry points into the matrix. One is constantly in a system of countervailing powers. It's exhausting, but it's remarkably effective.'*

This, then, is one of those very rare organizations where people had no qualms about discussing power games. Generally, the norm is to speak approvingly of consensus and the general interest. Here, politics was what drove things forward. The word 'culture' took on its full meaning, shedding its customary, honey-tongued complacency. It expressed an uncommon sense of liberty and lack of inhibition in grasping the political dimension of the decision-making process. It was not integrated into the company; it 'was' the company. Needless to say, this political aspect held sway to the detriment of clarity. This company was and remained a fuzzy organization both in the way its increasingly complex structures functioned and in the uncertainty surrounding the application of decisions, which were rarely formalized and spelt out. These were, and had to be, 'understood' and they were implemented as and when circumstances required it.

From that moment on, the skein unravelled effortlessly: complexity, fuzziness and the political dimension were handled via the networks. These had grown up with the passage of time and chance encounters. They assisted in providing the knowledge of whom to turn to, with whom to forge alliances in order to reach a decision, where to turn for the right information – all key resources in a world that thrived on its day-to-day approach to things. As one 'long-time' employee put it:

> *'What has changed over the last ten years? Perhaps that we are more factual and more results-driven, whereas before we were more subjective, more rhetorical. But we are every bit as network-oriented as we used to be.'*

At this point, it hardly comes as a surprise to note that, as in the previous cases, this organization depended heavily on people interacting. In fact, it was a reciprocal dependency, and it was not possible to rise to the highest echelons unless one had shown that one had understood the rules of the game. Of course, this meant everything depended more on people than on rules, procedures or structures, but these people were far from free to do as they pleased and how they pleased. They expressed their qualities within a 'regulated' system, and that was what prevented the 'fuzziness' from ever descending into anarchy. This accounted for the incessant mobility within the company, constantly switching people around, calling in others and moving the remainder, in response to opportunities arising within the company's very animated internal jobs market. If an employee wished to get ahead, they had to 'sell' themselves and impress upon others how necessary they were. Two interviewees spontaneously commented on this point:

> *'Obviously, when it comes to moving people around, the bosses theoretically don't have the right to do it without telling us [human resources]. But I'm not bothered about that if it's just a question of respecting some*

rule. I want more. I want them to consult me because they're really interested in what I have to say and because there's some real value added for them.'

'I try to bring in entrepreneurs above all. It's useful in this relatively informal environment. One's got to be able to live autonomously and impose oneself.'

The 'human resources' function, meanwhile, needed to be able to impose its know-how and constantly needed to demonstrate that it had this know-how. It might appear to be sidelined, at first glance, since all decisions were made by the 'operational' staff, and provided the end-results were satisfactory... Consequently, some interviewees stated somewhat radically that they expected nothing from the HR people and that if they wanted a change, they relied first and foremost on their own networks before getting the HR department to approve their decision. This was undeniably true, but the reality was rather more complicated. There was a clear and hefty bias in favour of operations, and the support functions were left to fend for themselves in the absence of any rules to do it for them. In other words, they functioned in a market, and their best hope of asserting themselves was by providing a very high standard of service. It was by presenting itself as a resource (and not as a bureaucratic constraint, as had so often been the case) for the operational employees that the HR department had gained 'acceptance', something that is illustrated in this interview excerpt:

'HR has a useful role to play in making suggestions. It can try to exert influence and above all it provides support, with training in particular. But at the end of the day, of course, it's the operational people who decide.'

Nevertheless, this function had had to become more professional, under the pressure of acquisitions in particular and of the need to integrate them without triggering a rush for the exits by the most talented people. It had therefore been necessary to separate the assessment of performance from mere arbitrary decisions – as had been the case until recently, although this was not a problem – to put it on a more formal footing. This was essential to ensuring that people from elsewhere had the feeling that they were joining a company with a sense of 'fairness'. It took this change in its stride, with no revolution in its mode of operation. One executive told me:

> *'What has changed, too, is the assessment of performance. Before, things were done orally, and there were people who took that pretty badly. Today, we treat people more fairly. So our hiring methods have improved, and we now have a fully-fledged training policy.'*

An original organization, where life is tough

Thus, what role did senior management play in this permanently thrusting environment? Certainly not to take sudden decisions applicable across the board! Being a boss in this environment can prove to be a very vague notion, when someone has the market knowledge to guarantee healthy sales results. To coin a phrase, in this company the senior managers played second fiddle to the market. But they were not inactive: remember, the force driving this magnificent machine was permanent confrontation. Nor was anarchy permitted to reign. The 'boss' (of the division, the brand or the region) organized this, acting as referee and observing how involved each of his subordinates was, serving timely reminders of this. This refereeing function could very quickly rise far up the chain of command. The different echelons listened and tried to narrow differences, and if no agreement were possible, the highest echelon made the final decision. In fact, the different management layers were far busier reconciling positions than issuing orders or seeking to dominate. So this was an open system that let everyone make his point. It naturally implied 'sanctions' (there was a well-established practice of 'shunting' people aside), which ensured that 'politicization' did not degenerate into pure power struggles disconnected from the 'business'.

The result was the progressive emergence of a highly original 'architecture', made up of networks, politics and trade-offs around authentic knowledge of the market. Clearly, here, we cannot say that the company stood on one side and its market on the other: the two were closely intertwined, and the need to stay close to the market at all times meant that all of the deviations described throughout of this book were avoided.

Having said that, it was clearly neither easy nor restful to work in an environment like this. Standing back, this firm could be said to have anticipated what the others are now starting to perceive in the early years of this century: to be effective, one needs to 'kill off' internal monopolies, introduce a high degree of cooperation (more realistically called 'confrontation' here) and develop more areas and opportunities for negotiation. But there is no getting away from the fact that in this company things were tough, sometimes very tough, and this was increasingly becoming the case. In the following quote an executive reflected with some bitterness on the situation:

> *'The way the firm works has unquestionably grown cumbersome. I'm not sure our chairman gets to meet the young product managers today, the way it used to be. It hasn't been so for about ten years, and the lower levels no longer understand what's going on at the top. As a result, it's gone from being a pleasure to being a duty. Today the pleasure is more and more limited.'*

What this was leading to was the more or less pronounced 'weariness' that results in a system where confrontation rules. Not only does one need to be strong to survive it, but those arriving late, after having experienced something very different, have little chance of success-fully integrating. It was part of the company's tradition to accept cases of burn-out, handling them as and when they arose, with no attempt to induce feelings of guilt. The company was adept at 'removing' an executive from a position after over-lengthy exposure. Some managers took charge of this unofficially. However, while the system remained unchanged in essence, the organization had grown exponentially in size, and thus in number and complexity. It will presumably become increasingly difficult to preserve this individual, qualitative and humane approach to personnel management.

What we have just described is a body of coherent, very well-articulated practices, which together formed the key to the success of this company. This is not surprising: since the end of the last century, a handful of authors[8] have sought (not very successfully) to draw attention to the primacy of the organizational factor in the success of companies: everyone has heard them, but no one has listened. What was surprising in this company was both the originality and the permanence of its mode of functioning: *plus ça change, plus c'est la même chose*, this time for the greater good of all.

Conclusion

We have arrived at the end of a series of curious journeys through a strange world – a contrasting world above all, one that resists simplistic, partisan interpretations, the kind that only understand what they presume to know already. The first lesson to be drawn from these visits to such different places is the permanence of the discussion. We come back here to the question posed by Taylorism, namely: *should an organization that produces goods and services and then markets them be scientific or human?* If it is scientific, as once dreamt of by SWO,[9] and which processes now seek to reproduce, then it can break free from people, their moods, their ups and downs, and their unpredictability. Moreover, being 'scientific', it is not open to dispute, barring dishonesty (grounds for exclusion) or mental disorder (leading many people to psychiatric hospitals).[10]

We have jettisoned that kind of vision. But it is the same distrust of work that finds expression today in the 'procedure-driven madness' and blind faith in processes,[11] to make sure that 'things work as they ought to and (that) people do what one would like them to do', which is the simplest and most telling definition of what is known as 'management'. But make no mistake: if a 'revamped' Taylorism is making a major comeback today, this is because the undisputed and growing harshness of work is prompting fears of the damage withdrawal can wreak. Clearly, companies face an accumulation of handicaps: what they 'let slip' yesterday – because it was deemed unimportant (a question of managerial sloth) and because the captive customer had no choice but to agree to pay the cost of these deviations – must now be recaptured, just when more and more people are coming to view work as repellent. Talk about getting the timing wrong! After losing their grip on work, organizations have even less confidence in it: bad habits have taken root, and in any case what is on offer is pretty unappealing. Thus, attention has turned to constraint, or to the elimination of work pure and simple.

We have seen the havoc constraint can wreak, with smart actors manipulating organizations, exploiting every weakness in systems of control that have become so erratic and contradictory that they end up controlling nothing. I have even suggested to executives at a seminar, who complained of the pressures of too many KPIs,[12] that they should demand more of them, as that would give them greater freedom. We have seen the creation of non-fuzzy but confusing abstract universes disconnected from reality, which only bureaucracies can navigate. We have seen the mad rush towards scrupulously defining every kind of activity in terms of processes, even though this renders their conclusion impossible other than through reliance on the goodwill of actors – who drive a hard bargain for it. Companies are still on the road to a veritable management disaster, driven by the diabolical marriage of bureaucrats, their mouths watering at the prospect of ever more pervasive processes, and managers primarily concerned with covering their own backs yet gradually losing control over what is happening on their watch.

It is not just control they are losing, which is already a problem in itself, but also, above all, efficacy. While introducing ever more rigid processes, all these companies dream of the flexibility they sorely need in order to thrive in economic conditions that have never been in such a state of flux. This is because the reason why one needs an organization capable of adapting swiftly, without having to undertake a thorough overhaul of these pointless regulations and replacing them with others that are just as pointless, is that these companies' businesses too are changing very quickly. Just to take an example: how many people realize that two large corporations, IBM and Accenture, are now in the process of 'cross-breeding'? The former, International Business *Machines* (sic!), has sold its personal computers business to a Chinese firm and is fast evolving into a pure services provider; at Accenture (the successor to Andersen Consulting), the share of consulting in its business portfolio is declining steadily, as it comes to manage its clients' ever-expanding computer resources. How can one acquire the necessary adaptability without reliance on people?

As for the elimination of work, this is not quite what Jeremy Rifkin had in mind.[13] It is the outcome of the widespread deployment of all those technologies that exclude work from the production of goods and services. In countries such as France – unlike the United States, for example – everything that is automated is 'good'. Anyone expressing the slightest reservations is dismissed as being hostile to progress. But progress, in our case, is what replaces men by machines, not for the wellbeing of the worker, who is driven out of a job, or even that of the client, who is often confused by the process, but for that of the people 'in charge', who are thus relieved of the task of managing that intractable thing, human labour.

The vicious circle of work and employment

Taken to extremes, this logic can drag a society into a self-sustaining vicious circle of work and employment problems. The less one trusts work, the more one seeks to reduce one's dependence on it by continuously reducing its place in the production process. The more this place is reduced, the more one fuels the problem of employment, for the younger generations especially. Work is no more an area of inter-generational excellence than is the management of our debt. Responsibility for this is very much a shared one, between companies on the one hand, which, having neglected the problem, now quail before the scale of the task of getting people to work, and the trade unions on the other, clinging to sometimes outlandish (deathly, in the words of one union) acquired rights that have outlived their usefulness. The overriding mood is one of 'Every man for himself, and God for all!' except, in all likelihood, for those coming after.

This explains why I asked whether it is possible to do things differently. Fortunately, a few examples do come to hand to push the door slightly ajar. I would like to open them a little wider. In order to do so, it is necessary to constantly bear in mind the distinction between structure and organization, something not always clear in the minds of most chief executives. However, it has been around for a long time![14] Nevertheless, once this is understood, and once the idea is firmly assimilated that the term 'organization' refers to the business of organizing real and daily ways of working, deciding and living together, to cut a long story short, organizational flexibility refers to the flexibility of work and not to changes in structures. The countless 'reorganizations', for which read 'rearranging the company's jigsaw puzzle', have never prevented things from going on as before. People are well and truly the crux of the matter, not 'all the rest', which is merely the company's façade.

Similarly, where activities are concerned, can we dispense with the ridiculous distinction between 'hard' and 'soft', as some immature chief executives mindlessly intone? The former is assumed to designate what counts (finance, business), while the latter refers to anything vaguely human. This is an intellectually lazy approach, with dangerous practical implications. It has been demonstrated many times that the tougher the competition in increasingly open markets, the less it is products as such that make the difference. Once again, it is 'organization', in other words people and the way they work, which holds the key to the contemporary equation of how to do better with less. In a word, the message for all lovers of simplistic distinctions is that it is the organization that is 'hard'.

Now we can talk seriously. I travelled the world during the course of 2009 and 2010, visiting some of the largest firms in all sectors in order to gain an insight into how they were going about growing their businesses.[15] They all described their initiatives in terms of organizational innovations. All explained and showed that the difference between themselves and their competitors from all quarters, including unexpected ones, lay in their capacity to invent new, flexible, responsive and adaptive ways of working, far from the cumbersome procedures seen in the traditional business world. They had discovered, or rediscovered, that fostering an open market in skills was far less costly and far more effective than having to go through unwieldy hierarchical structures and dense processes, which resulted in increased 'transaction costs'.

It is worth noting that innovation, in the sense of devising different ways of working, comes from the United States. It is amusing, sometimes, to see the entire Western business community turning like a single man towards the emerging countries, arguing that that is where tomorrow's markets are, while ignoring that the organizations of tomorrow are being invented elsewhere. There too, the herd instinct is at work.

Some keys to the new organization

These new organizations can be summed up briefly in a few key points. The first is obvious and has already been mentioned in this book: everything must be focused on the search for the most fully integrated solution possible for the client. We are witnessing the twilight of 'pure' product selling, as evidenced – to cite a timely example – by the switch from cellphones to smartphones. Customers are increasingly being sold bundles of products and solutions, and they are increasingly interested in the service rather than in support, except where 'design' is a factor. This notion of solutions is splitting up traditional organizations, mired in individualism, turf battles and strict obedience to hierarchies. The question here is no longer one of formalism or decorum but of networking the competencies needed to formulate a response to the client as quickly as possible, wherever those competencies happen to be. That is what companies like Cisco or Hewlett Packard call 'virtual communities'.

Needless to say, the 'components' of these solutions may be 'technical' in nature, but this never comes up as a major issue. Technical aspects, today, will do as General de Gaulle said of administrative staff: they will do what they are told. On the other hand, arranging these different items is a question of organization and its members' capacity to cooperate quickly and well. 'Transversality', i.e., overcoming barriers between departments and functions, is the core concept driving these new organizations. But this should not be seen as a process – yet another one. It depends on the company's capacity to foster cooperative behaviour, not by constraint or moral rhetoric, but by its understanding of the wellsprings of collective action, of what will give the actors an 'interest' in working together.

On this central issue, we must jettison managerial fads and abstract proclamations. In particular, the axiom that 'everything that has been said, decided or stated will be done' is worthy of Pontius Pilate washing his hands of the matter. Consequently, we need to go on seeking innovative solutions and ask what it really takes to create 'communities of interest'. This calls forth modes of human and financial management that are genuinely conducive to the emergence of these communities and not merely to the desire for their emergence. We finally shatter the academic canons of good management. This may imply counting the same thing several times over, for example. I can already see chief financial officers sitting up with a start at this. And yet how can one simultaneously expect the greatest possible number of actors to work together to devise ever more complex solutions for their clients while telling them each will receive only a slice of the cake, and a very carefully measured one at that? That would merely close down the perspectives instead of broadening them; to keep all of the cake for themselves, each of the actors will strive relentlessly to reduce the number of participants. Instead of possible cooperation, we end up with certain exclusion. So let's go for multiple counting and shadow profit and loss statements, and for any other form of counting capable of making actors want to go on expanding the size of the cake.

All of this brings the question of trust centre-stage again, which includes the question of the rules of the game and hence ethics. The question is no longer about asking the actors to refrain from 'doing just anything' to grow the business, which would be especially hypocritical in a world where the performance of individuals is assessed with ever-greater frequency. The question, rather, is how to help them build a less uncertain, more predictable working environment, one that allows each individual to rely a little more on others, with no need for procedures and processes that increase complexity instead of simplifying things. Cisco, Barclays, Itau Banco (Brazil's leading bank) and Accenture, to cite just a handful of companies embodying these innovations, are reporting highly positive results. I am not just talking about economic results but also about decisive progress in the capacity to get people to work differently and to believe in themselves by ridding them of all that artificially complicates their work and ends up making everyone cynical and irresponsible. There is nothing inevitable in all this, and that is where hope lies.

Notes

Introduction

1. Christian Morel, *Le mal chronique de la connaissance ordinaire sur l'entreprise* (*The Chronic Disorder of 'Ordinary' Knowledge about the Firm*), Annales des Mines, 1992, pp. 71–3.
2. See, for example, Philippe Askenazy, *Les désordres du travail: enquête sur un nouveau productivisme* (*Disorder in the Workplace: An Inquiry into a New Productivism*), Collection La République des Idées, Editions du Seuil, 2004. See also the work of Jacques de Bandt, a specialist in industrial economics, or Christophe Dejour, a psychoanalyst and psychiatrist, and Chair in the Psychology of Labour at the CNAM.
3. Olivier Tirmarche, *Au-delà de la souffrance au travail : clés pour un autre management*, Odile Jacob, 2010.
4. François Dupuy, *The Customer's Victory. From Corporation to Co-operation*, Macmillan Business, 1999.
5. This concerns the reversal of the flow of wealth in the world from the mid-1970s onwards. Before then, countries in the West built their 'welfare states' on cheap raw materials from the countries of the South. Today, these same countries are building their development on wealth that they themselves are levying from the countries of the North, thanks to their very low production costs.
6. This is one way of interpreting the chapter on this topic in Hubert Bonin's *Les Tabous de Bordeaux (The Taboos of Bordeaux)*, Le Festin éditeurs, 2010. See Chapter 5 on the Bordeaux wine industry's business model.
7. See *'Le sous-travail, un fléau qui gangrène la société française'* ('Underwork, a Scourge Eating Away at French Society'), interview published in *Les Echos*, 23 May 2009.
8. Often it is not until the French *Cour des Comptes* (State Audit Court) turns its attention to an issue (e.g., air traffic controllers) that the phenomenon emerges in broad daylight, before being swiftly swept under the carpet. Such topics are subject to a veritable 'code of silence'. Should a 'treacherous' insider spill the beans, he will instantly draw unanimous condemnation and the content will be studiously ignored.
9. See, for example, François Dupuy, *La Fatigue des Elites (The Elites are Weary)*, Collection La République des Idées, Le Seuil, 2005. David Courpasson and Jean-Claude Thoenig, *Quand les cadres se rebellent (When Executives Rebel)*, Vuibert, 2008.
10. According to Max Weber.

1 We Have Let Work 'Slip'

1. François Dupuy and Jean-Claude Thoenig, *La Loi du Marché: l'électroménager en France, aux Etats Unis et au Japon*, L'Harmattan, 1980.
2. Corinne Maier, *Hello Laziness!: Why Hard Work Doesn't Pay*, Orion Publishing Group, 2005.
3. Nor does one need to be a sociologist to be convinced of this.
4. Louis Chauvel, *Les Classes Moyennes à la Dérive (The Middle Classes Adrift), Collection La République des Idées*, Le Seuil, 2006. See Chapter 3 in particular.
5. It is probably this increasing harshness of working conditions that explains why it is no longer the butt of comedians' jokes. Except where transport is concerned – where under-work can cause considerable inconvenience – there is a consensus in our societies that if certain categories of worker find ways to escape the rigours of ever-tougher and more burdensome working conditions, then so much the better for them.
6. This study was carried out in 2008.
7. See Chapter 5.
8. Like other firms, this firm had conducted a number of (discreet) studies on productivity differentials between tenured and temporary staff. However, the findings had been carefully filed away, as is often the case, being felt to be a source of potential 'labour unrest'.
9. François Dupuy, *Sharing Knowledge*, Palgrave Macmillan, 2004.
10. We conducted two studies here, in 2007 and 2008.
11. Simone Weil, *La condition ouvrière*, Collection Idées, NRF, éditions Gallimard, 1951.
12. I owe this felicitous expression to Michel Crozier.
13. C. Durand and A. Touraine, 'Le rôle compensateur des agents de maîtrise', *Sociologie du Travail* (1970), 2, 113–39.
14. This study was carried out in 2007.
15. In fact, it was the unions that overrode the strikers' ballot and called an end to the strike.

2 Silo Organizations and their Unwanted Side-Effects

1. See Chapter 5
2. This study was carried out in 2007.
3. For instance, suppliers responded to calls for tenders by quoting unbeatably low prices, knowing full well that the final demand would bear little relation to the initial invitation, this having been drafted by a unit unfamiliar with the unit that expressed the need. That is what is meant by 'making the client pay the price of integration'.
4. This study was carried out in 2008.
5. C. Michaud and J.C. Thoenig, *Making Organization and Strategy Compatible*, Palgrave Macmillan, 2003.

3 We've Let the Customer Get Away

1. This study was conducted in 2007.
2. Brazil, Russia, India and China.
3. The study concerned seven countries, in Europe, Asia, North America and South America.
4. Robert B. Reich, *The Work of Nations: Preparing Ourselves for 21st Century Capitalism*, Alfred A. Knopf, 1992.
5. This study was carried out in 2007.

4 Sacrificing the Front-line Managers

1. 'Toyotism' is a form of work organization of which the Japanese engineer Taiichi Ono is considered to be the father. The formal application of 'Toyotism' in Toyota's plants is known as the Toyota Production System (TPS). The system gives priority to its operatives in the quest for best quality at the lowest cost.
2. This study was carried out in 2008.
3. This study was carried out in 2008.
4. This study was carried out in 2006.

5 Integration and Processes: A Marriage Made in Hell

1. Erhard Friedberg, *Le Pouvoir et la Règle. Dynamiques de l'action organisée*, Le Seuil, 1993.
2. Translator's note: a rule introduced into the French Constitution in 1995.
3. Cf. the case presented below, p. 119.
4. This study was carried out in 2008.
5. Much has been written about the role of trust in management. The best article, in my view, is by Ellen M. Whitener, Susan E. Brobt, M. Audrey Korsgaard and Jon N. Werner, 'Managers as Initiators of Trust: An Exchange Relationship Framework for Understanding Managerial Trustworthy Behaviour', *Academy of Management Review* (1999), 23(3), 513–30.
6. This study was carried out in 2007.

6 Trust Destroyed, Trust Rebuilt

1. Michel Crozier, *The Bureaucratic Phenomenon*, University of Chicago Press, 1964.
2. On the notion of ethics and its bearing on management, see David Pastoriza, Miguel A. Arino and Johan E. Ricart, 'Ethical Managerial Behavior as an Antecedent of Organizational Social Capital', *Journal of Business Ethics* (2008), 78(3), 329–41.
3. This study was carried out in 2010.

4. This study was carried out in 2010.
5. The notion of 'contract worker' in what is still a public sector agency may be misleading. Here the term refers to people who did not have civil servant status, but who were on open-ended contracts.
6. These 'modular' rounds could be broken up and distributed among other postal workers if one of them was on leave or absent, or if the traffic was lighter, for example, during the holidays.
7. There is nothing mercantile in the notion of 'buying a delivery round'. It is simply a matter of gaining sufficient seniority to be definitively assigned a round, which means graduating from the situation of a replacement postal worker to that of permanent postal worker.
8. The 'CYA syndrome'.

7   The Difficulty of Changing Endogenous Organizations

1. I refer here to the work of James March, Herbert Simon, Mancur Olson, Thomas Schelling and, of course, Michel Crozier.
2. This study was carried out in 2008.
3. This expression was coined by Chris Argyris in *Knowledge for Action. A Guide to Overcoming Barriers to Organizational Change*, Jossey-Bass, 1993.
4. This study was carried out in 2010.

8   Simplicity, Trust and Communities of Interest: Can Things Be Done Differently?

1. See, for example, Rosabeth Moss Kanter, 'Transforming Giants: What Kind of Company Makes It Its Business to Make the World a Better Place?', *Harvard Business Review*, January 2008, 43–52.
2. This study was carried out in 2008.
3. The legendary former head of General Electric.
4. Translator's note: regulation, in this context, refers to a self-adjusting system, not to regulations.
5. This study was carried out in 2009.
6. Jack Trout with Steve Rivkin, *The Power of Simplicity: A Management Guide to Cutting Through the Nonsense of Doing Things Right*, McGraw-Hill, 1999.
7. This study was carried out in 2008.
8. Rosabeth Moss Kanter and Peter Drucker in particular.
9. Scientific Work Organization or scientific organization of work.
10. Remember, Lenin was an early admirer of Taylor, as he wrote to Rosa Luxemburg.
11. There is a very abundant literature on processes, chiefly in the English-speaking world. Examples include John Jeston and Johan Nelis, *Business Process Management: Practical Guidelines to Successful Implementations*, Butterworth-Heinemann, 2006. See also Ravi Amipindi, Sunil Chopra,

Sudhakr D. Deshmikh, Jan A. Van Nieghem and Eithan Zemel, *Managing Business Process Flows: Principles of Operations Management*, 2nd edn, Prentice Hall, 2003.

12. Key Performance Indicators. For a detailed insight into the use of this method of assessment, see David Parmenter, *Key Performance Indicators: Developing, Implementing, and Using Winning KPIs*, John Wiley & Sons, 2010.

13. Jeremy Rifkin, *The End of Work: The Decline of the Global Labor Force and the Dawn of the Post-Market Era*, Putnam Publishing Group, 1995.

14. See, for example, the famous article published 30 years ago by R. Waterman, Jr., T. Peters and J.R. Phillips, 'Structure is not Organization', *Business Horizons* (1980), 23(3), 14–26.

15. I would particularly like to thank GDF-Suez University for giving me this opportunity.

Index